MYTHS, GODS, AND RITUALS OF AZTEC MYTHOLOGY

MYTHS, GODS, AND RITUALS OF AZTEC MYTHOLOGY

Before the First Sun

MATTHEW TORRES

MIAMI

Copyright © 2025 by Matthew Torres.
Published by Mango Publishing, a division of Mango Publishing Group, Inc.

Cover Design: Elina Diaz
Cover Photo/Illustrations: Stock.adobe.com/naihoet, stock.adobe.com/Anatoliy
Interior Illustrations: Stock.adobe.com/Juanpa Duque
Layout & Design: Elina Diaz

Mango is an active supporter of authors' rights to free speech and artistic expression in their books. The purpose of copyright is to encourage authors to produce exceptional works that enrich our culture and our open society.

Uploading or distributing photos, scans or any content from this book without prior permission is theft of the author's intellectual property. Please honor the author's work as you would your own. Thank you in advance for respecting our author's rights.

For permission requests, please contact the publisher at:
Mango Publishing Group
5966 South Dixie Highway, Suite 300
Miami, FL 33143
info@mango.bz

For special orders, quantity sales, course adoptions and corporate sales, please email the publisher at sales@mango.bz. For trade and wholesale sales, please contact Ingram Publisher Services at customer.service@ingramcontent.com or +1.800.509.4887.

Myths, Gods, and Rituals of Aztec Mythology: Before the First Sun

Library of Congress Cataloging-in-Publication number: 2025942995
ISBN: (p) 978-1-68481-864-8, (e) 978-1-68481-865-5
BISAC category code: SOC011000 SOCIAL SCIENCE / Folklore & Mythology

TABLE OF CONTENTS

Introduction   **13**

Part 1 The War   **17**

Chapter 1 Duality   19

Chapter 2 Order and Chaos   23

Chapter 3 The God of Wind   27

Chapter 4 The Gods of War   31

Chapter 5 The Gods of Life   37

Chapter 6 The Star Demons   43

Chapter 7 The Gods of Magic   47

Chapter 8 The Gods of Death   57

Part 2 The Age of Gods   **61**

Chapter 9 The Thirteen Heavens   63

Chapter 10 Love, Death, and Magic   67

Chapter 11 The Tonantzin   71

Chapter 12 The Weeping Woman   75

Chapter 13 The Wild God Hunts the Deer Woman   79

Chapter 14 Arrows and Claws   85

Chapter 15 The Shield Goddess   89

Chapter 16 The Trial   93

Part 3 The Divine Flower War — 97

Chapter 17 Shield vs. Arrows — 101

Chapter 18 Storm vs. Death — 107

Chapter 19 Claws vs. Sin — 111

Chapter 20 Magic vs. Bones — 115

Chapter 21 The Deal — 119

Chapter 22 Shield vs. Claws — 123

Chapter 23 Grudge Match — 127

Chapter 24 The Final Battle — 131

Chapter 25 And the Winner Is... — 137

Part 4 A History Lesson — 141

Chapter 26 The Aztec Didn't Call Themselves the Aztec — 143

Chapter 27 "Savages Living in Trees" — 147

Chapter 28 Blood on Their Hands — 151

Chapter 29 The Massacres — 155

Chapter 30 They Thought They Were Gods (Except They Didn't) — 157

Chapter 31 Mythology That Contradicts — 159

Chapter 32 Learning the Language — 161

Conclusion — 167

About the Author — 171

INTRODUCTION

"The truth is told best when it is told as a story."

—Hélène Elizabeth Louise Amélie Paula Dolores Poniatowska Amor

Aztec myths were never meant to be read like history books. If this book were filled with myths, recounted directly as a textbook would, it would comprise only a few pages, and most stories would read like this:

> In the Era of the First Sun, Quetzalcoatl and Tezcatlipoca fought. Quetzalcoatl won. The end.

Why did they fight? We don't know. How did they fight? We don't know. Where did they fight? We don't know. *But*—we can speculate! And that's exactly what this book will do. It will take history and mythology and add story through educated speculation.

Why did they fight? Quetzalcoatl was the God of Justice, and Tezcatlipoca was being mean to the Giants (yes, the Aztec had Giants). How did they fight? Tezcatlipoca carried with him the Smoking Mirror, an obsidian mirror seething with magic. Quetzalcoatl had the power of an ancient primordial deity coursing through his veins. Where did they fight? In the Thirteen Heavens, where the gods made their homes.

Now, with context clues from mythology, we have a picture of two powerhouse gods fighting. The God of Magic summoning forces of chaos to battle a gigantic, feathered dragon-snake who breathes wind so powerful it obliterates whole forests. Two powerful forces fighting for the fate of the world, both believing they're right, and with a cohesive narrative tying it all together. That's what this book is, and what other books on Aztec mythology aren't.

See, it's one thing to tell history, but it's another thing entirely to make history entertaining. Trust me, I was a substitute teacher for years, and most of the videos I made as a content creator were about history. History can be made entertaining, and that is what this book is about.

Aztec history, especially mythology, was passed down in fractured pieces. What little remains is filtered through colonial accounts, rewritten by friars, mistranslated by outsiders, and shaped by the trauma of conquest. For every surviving sentence, there are pages lost to fire, censorship, or forgetfulness. And while many modern historians seek to piece it back together, this book seeks something different: to breathe life back into those fragments.

And let's be honest: most mythology books are either academic and dry or so loose with the facts they barely qualify as mythology. This book lives in the space between—rigorous in research, but imaginative in spirit. These are myths retold through a storyteller's lens, with every effort made to stay rooted in the surviving lore, while also building bridges where the records go silent.

Is the book historically accurate? Absolutely. It took me years and years and dozens of books and countless hours of research to compile the knowledge that fills this book. What's more, as you will read in the history section, compiling the broken pieces of Aztec mythology wasn't an easy feat; there's so much contradiction and misinformation it becomes a maze, with many paths leading to dead ends.

Now, does this book take several liberties when telling the history? Without a doubt—but otherwise, frankly, it would be boring. This book follows in the footsteps of other creative works that have done similar things: taking nonfiction history and presenting it in fictional fashion.

Hamilton by Lin-Manuel Miranda retold American history (but with song).

1984 by George Orwell was inspired by the Soviet Union (but with animals).

Game of Thrones by George R. R. Martin was inspired by the real-life War of the Roses and took several inspirations from history throughout the world.

These are all fictional stories inspired—sometimes very closely—by real history. Now, this book isn't some grand fictional Aztec adventure, though one day I might write that. This story is taking history and adding flavor and excitement, all in a way that does not veer too far from the historical facts.

This book is not about inventing a new mythology. It's about honoring an old one. It's a restoration project, a mythological mural made from surviving tiles and thoughtful reconstructions. This is mythology retold through storytelling what was once whispered in smoke and sung in temples, now brought to life again on the page. This is the story before the First Sun.

PART 1

THE WAR

Aztec mythology gives us glimpses of gods, monsters, and cosmic cycles, but very little survives that explains how it all began. There is no surviving myth that tells us how the gods came to be, how the great Chaos was defeated, or what the world looked like before the First Sun. We know the destination, but the journey remains unknown and unwritten.

In Part 1, we will attempt to tell that missing story. It is not a replacement for Aztec mythology, but a respectful imagining of what could fill the space between fragments. This is a fictional retelling of the birth of the gods, the rise of the Earth, and the path that led to the First Sun.

CHAPTER 1
DUALITY

Before anything had a name, and before creation itself existed, there was Ometeotl (Oh-Meh-Tee-Oat). Ometeotl was not a god, but a Primordial. It had no free will, nor destiny in life. Ometeotl simply existed, and from it, all things were made. All things, in twos, always. Fire and water, life and death, war and peace. From this duality came the formation of the universe and everything within it.

From its heart beat cosmic change, and with each beat, more Primordials were born. With one breath, Ometeotl sang a song of purpose and gave these purposes to each Primordial. Then it weaved from its body its blood and life, and gave duality to all things in the universe. Life, Purpose, Duality.

Life cannot be stopped once started, and so Ometeotl created more and more. It created more life, and more death, and more Primordials, and more chaos. Over and over it created, endlessly, without any notion of stopping.

The first echo of this heartbeat came with the Primordial of Magic. Magic was neither good nor evil, and it was powerful, yet fragile. The things Magic could do were numerous and awe-inspiring. Yet, the magic could only go so far as where Ometeotl found itself. To carry Magic across the cosmos, Ometeotl created the Primordial of Wind, and on this wind, magic swept throughout the land. Hand in hand, heart with heart, Magic and Wind filled every corner of every section of every part of the universe. The two Primordials danced across the black nothingness, filling the emptiness with sparks of life and hope.

Once magic was spread throughout the cosmos, the next to be created was the Primordial of Life, a being so pure and so beautiful, all worshipped and looked upon Life in awe. Yet, with all things living, Death must follow, and so the Primordial of Death came soon after. Death did not hate Life, nor did Life hate Death. They saw each other as necessary, and felt that Life was given meaning only because Death would one day follow. If all things lived forever, the joy of life would vanish.

Once Life and Death had formed, Conflict followed. The Primordial of Conflict created tension in the universe, between all things, for growth can only happen when adversity is put forth. Yet, not all things grow this way, and certainly not all things grow under constant conflict, and so the Primordial of Peace balanced Conflict. Conflict was needed, of course, but all things in due time. Not everything grows overnight, nor can change happen when only complacency is present.

By the hand and will of Ometeotl, many dozens of pairs of Primordials formed Land and Sea, Fire and Water, Predator and Prey, Storm and Sea, Fear and Courage, Silence and Sound. Eventually, over a hundred Primordials had formed, and from them, the universe began to take shape. They became like threads in a great tapestry, each crossing the other, forming the patterns of stars, the rhythm of seasons, the very breath of existence. For a time, all was well, until it wasn't.

Ometeotl

Pronounced: [Oh-meh-teh-ohtl]

Meaning: Two God

God of: Duality

Appearance: Ometeotl is rarely depicted anthropomorphically in codices. Instead, Ometeotl exists as a dual force.

Fun Fact: There is scholarly debate on whether Ometeotl was actively worshipped, or existed only as a theological idea. Codices do not show temples or rituals to Ometeotl the way they do for other deities, reinforcing its abstract role.

History: Unlike the later gods of the Aztec pantheon, Ometeotl was not worshipped in temples or through rituals, but existed as a metaphysical principle beyond human comprehension. Ometeotl is sometimes described as the source of all life, thought, and balance in the universe. Though not widely mentioned in surviving codices, later Aztec and post-conquest sources elevate Ometeotl as the philosophical root of existence.

CHAPTER 2
ORDER AND CHAOS

Ometeotl, on a mission to create a beautiful universe, forgot about one important rule. Ironically, that one rule was the principle to which Ometeotl owed its name: duality. Ometeotl had created all of these beautiful things, and all of these great powers, and from all these beautiful and powerful things came Order. An order of powerful primordial deities, all working together to create. But if there was a great Order, so too must there have been a great Chaos.

The scales of the universe were tipped so heavily in the favor of beauty and love and life that a natural course correction had to be made. A force was created that was singular in its power and intention, and as strong as the force to which it opposed. If the universe was overwhelmingly Order, then the Chaos created to tip the balance must be even greater than the Order. This Chaos formed and shaped into a monstrous being, and that being was given a name: Cipactli.

Too busy with their own destinies and designs, the Primordials did not realize Cipactli had arrived and spread until it was too late. They did not realize all the Chaos that had been growing right under their noses, and when they did, it was simply too late.

The Primordials who stayed and fought were defeated. Those who ran were caught. Those who hid were found. The Chaos consumed all, twisted good into bad, and flooded the universe. It poisoned all, cursed the rest, and created horrors in the universe that even nightmares feared.

Cipactli was only as powerful as the Primordials, for it was the echo of their Order. But whereas the Primordials were many, Cipactli was singular. The Chaos had what the Primordials did not: unity. Ironic, isn't it?

Ometeotl looked upon Cipactli with disgust and horror, and knew that if it were to defeat this monster, the Primordials must stand united. But this was easier said than done, for the Primordials had no free will. They had their destinies and fates tied to their missions. Life could only do one thing: create life. War could only cause war. Peace could only cause peace. They had no freedom or free will to do as they pleased.

And so the Chaos grew, larger and larger, until finally, Ometeotl was left with one singular decision. If the Primordials could not fight back, then they could no longer be Primordials. Ometeotl met with Cipactli, in front of the eyes of all the others, and it greeted the Chaos with open arms.

Chapter 2: Order and Chaos

Cipactli tore into Ometeotl with its endless mouths and endless claws, tearing the Primordial to pieces, until Ometeotl was so destroyed and without form, it had to tear itself in two. In that single moment, all of reality was changed.

The balance that held all things split. Not shattered, but separated entirely. Not destroyed, but changed from purpose. This change spread throughout the universe, into everything, and around everyone. The Primordials were split into two forces of duality, no longer Primordials, now gods.

The first to split itself was Ometeotl, who became the Gods of Duality, Ometecuhtli, and Omecihuatl. The Lord and Lady of Duality.

Cipactli was next, and the Chaos was broken into one singular whole and a nearly endless horde. A powerful individual monster continued being Cipactli, but the many mouths and many eyes and many endless stomachs each broke off, and fled into the vast space of the universe.

Though separated, they were no more or less deadly than they once had been. The Chaos tore holes in the fabric of reality, leaving behind scars we still see in the form of black holes and dying stars. They consumed planets and chewed on stars, and in every shadow, they waited for more to feast on. They lurked, they hid, and they waited.

Chaos did not roar. It whispered. And the gods answered it.

Cipactli

Pronounced: [See-pahk-tlee]

Meaning: Crocodile, Monster of Chaos

God of: Primordial Chaos, the Hunger, the Uncreated

Appearance: Cipactli is described in most sources as a massive crocodilian sea monster with multiple mouths across its body. It swims through the void between worlds, a fusion of earth, ocean, and night. In some tellings, Cipactli has no fixed form, shifting constantly, sprouting eyes and teeth wherever gods dare look.

Fun Fact: In the *Leyenda de los Soles*, Cipactli is described as having so many mouths that it could not eat without devouring itself.

History: Cipactli appears in early Mesoamerican myth not as a deity to be worshipped, but as a raw, foundational force that predates the gods themselves. In Aztec cosmology, Cipactli represents the untamed chaos from which the structured universe was carved. It was not born, but emerged as a necessity: if the world is made of order, then chaos must answer. Unlike most beings in the Aztec pantheon, Cipactli was never worshipped through temples or sacrifice; it was feared.

CHAPTER 3

THE GOD OF WIND

After Order and Chaos had come, Wind followed.

Ometecuhtli and Omecihuatl placed their hands together, and by their will the Primordial of Wind turned into the God of Wind, and unlike the others, who found a duality in their forms, Wind took only one form. It needed no second self, no dual reflection. It was perfect in its singularity. It was Quetzalcoatl, the Feathered Serpent.

Quetzalcoatl was vast. It moved like the tide of time and stretched from star to star. Its body shimmered with scales of emerald and gold, and its feathers caught the light of a sun that had not yet been born. Each scale bore a memory of the worlds to come, and each plume stirred the dust of unborn planets. Its breath stirred the stars into their constellations, and when it hissed, galaxies spun.

But Wind was never just air. Wind was direction. Wind was change. Wind was the force that carried life and death from one place to the next. It was the first traveler, the first messenger, the first hand to guide the world toward fate. Where Quetzalcoatl turned, so too turned the future.

Unlike the gods that came before and after, Quetzalcoatl did not take a weapon or cast a spell. It *was* its power. Every movement of its body shaped reality. Every flap of its wings whispered meaning into the void. Every twist of its spine unraveled chaos and rewrote it as balance.

Quetzalcoatl saw Cipactli as not just a beast, but a festering wound that would never stop bleeding. Some wounds can heal; others have to be excised from the body. This wound was only going to grow; it was a cancer, and to save the body, the cancer had to be removed. Though Quetzalcoatl did not hate Cipactli, it knew that it must fall.

Quetzalcoatl, not nearly as big but nearly as strong, slammed into Cipactli with all the force of movement there was in the universe. And Quetzalcoatl did not stop; it brought with it planets and stars and forced those too to crash into Cipactli.

Had Quetzalcoatl not had grace or a desire for peace, perhaps it could have ended the fight then. But when Cipactli screamed in pain, Quetzalcoatl hesitated. It cared about all life, and whether that life was good or evil, it didn't matter. This hesitation, however noble it was, would lead to his own downfall.

Cipactli grabbed onto Quetzalcoatl, stopped its movement, and tore it to pieces. Realizing its inevitable end, Quetzalcoatl halted all movement around Cipactli. It would never be allowed to move ever again, for all the force of the universe was pushing against it in every direction.

Quetzalcoatl wrapped its body around the Chaos and tied their destinies together. If Quetzalcoatl would fall, so too would Cipactli. As Cipactli thrashed, screamed, and cursed, Quetzalcoatl the Feathered Serpent held tighter, sacrificing its very soul to slow the destruction.

And then Quetzalcoatl died.

Its feathers fell like comets, streaking the dark with green fire. Its body crumbled to mist and memory. But from the last of its heart, something solid formed. A jade stone, perfectly round, still warm, glowing faintly with the breath of wind that would one day rise again.

That jade stone fell through the cosmos like a single tear. Where it landed, the others did not know.

Quetzalcoatl was the first god to die. But not the last.

Quetzalcoatl

Pronounced: [Keh-tsahl-KOH-ahtl]

Meaning: Feathered Serpent

God of: Wind, Direction, Wisdom

Appearance: A massive serpent with jeweled scales and iridescent feathers. Despite the notion of Quetzalcoatl being a flying snake, Quetzalcoatl did *not* have wings. One day, Quetzalcoatl would be reborn, and in that appearance, he would look human. Initially, however, he was a gigantic snake covered in feathers.

Fun Fact: The name Quetzalcoatl is actually a double entendre. While a direct translation is Quetzal Coatl, Feathered Serpent, those two words have dual meanings. *Quetzal* means "feathered," but it also means "wise." *Coatl* means "snake," but snakes are also a symbol of eternity. Therefore Quetzalcoatl is not just the Feathered Serpent, he is also the Wise Eternal. This makes sense, as he is also the God of Wisdom.

History: The Feathered Serpent motif is one of the oldest symbols of mythology in all of the Americas. Not only is it the oldest, it's one of the most widespread. All over the Americas we can find stories—stories that long predate the Aztec—about large feathered snakes, and they are always gods of wind and justice.

CHAPTER 4
THE GODS OF WAR

With Cipactli trapped, Ometecuhtli and Omecihuatl raced over to the Primordial of War, touched their hands upon its chest, and from it came two powerful Gods of War: Huitzilopochtli and Itzpapalotl. The Hummingbird of the Left, and the Obsidian Butterfly.

Huitzilopochtli came with the sun behind his back and fire in his chest. His steps left embers, his breath shook the skies, and he wanted one thing and one thing only: to wage war. The God of War was not one for strategy, nor one for dealings. He fought, and he fought, and when he was unsure what to do, he fought some more.

Where others studied, he struck. Where others questioned, he charged. His mind was simple but pure, for it desired only war. The hunger for war was never sated, and quite the opposite was true: the hunger to fight grew stronger with each battle. The more he fought, the more he needed to fight.

In the war against Cipactli, Huitzilopochtli was the first to charge. He did not wait for orders. He did not speak with the others. He saw the Chaos and leapt into action.

His power was unmatched, his rage unstoppable. He struck out with his fists and his feet and his teeth. He punched, kicked, and bit the Chaos. He needed no weapon, for he was the weapon, and Cipactli felt his destruction. Cipactli fought back, tearing at Huitzilopochtli, but it did not stop him. The God of War struck with all his might, beating and battering Cipactli.

He tore into Cipactli like a god possessed. He drove his feet into its side. He split its mouths open with his fists. He clawed at its eyes with his burning hands. He roared and bled and screamed until the Chaos itself trembled. The other gods watched in awe, for no being had ever fought with such reckless fury. No one had ever made Cipactli stagger.

But something stirred beneath the surface of Cipactli, something vast and quiet and waiting. Cipactli had many mouths, and many of them bit. But one mouth, deeper than the rest, was not meant for eating. It was meant for ending.

As Huitzilopochtli dove in for a final strike, his war cry rising louder than thunder, that horrible smiling mouth opened... and swallowed the God of War whole. In a single horrible moment, Huitzilopochtli was gone. But nothing truly ends.

The mouth of Cipactli coughed out a single feather. A hummingbird feather, so small it could be missed. So light, it did not fall, but floated. It drifted through the air, caught in a breeze that none could feel, and vanished into the sky.

One day, that feather would return. But not yet. Not now. Not while the war raged on.

Huitzilopochtli

Pronounced: [Weet-see-loh-POCH-tlee]

Meaning: Hummingbird of the South

God of: War, the Sun, Sacrifice, and the South

Appearance: Depicted with hummingbird feathers, often wearing a helmet shaped like a hummingbird's beak. His body is painted blue, with red splashes to symbolize blood and battle.

Fun Fact: Huitzilopochtli was one of the few gods in the Aztec pantheon whose worship required constant sacrifice. The Aztec believed his strength kept the sun moving, and without the blood of warriors, the sun would falter.

History: Revered as the patron deity of the Mexica, Huitzilopochtli was the driving force behind the Aztec's expansion and conquest. He represented both the spirit of warfare and the belief that struggle was necessary for life to continue. Though his name became synonymous with the sun, he was not gentle or warm; he was scorching, blinding, and unstoppable.

All the while Huitzilopochtli fought with relentless fury, his other half, Itzpapalotl, planned. Where the God of War was unmitigated raw destruction, the Goddess of War planned in advance. For all the strategies the God of War did not plan, the Goddess of War did.

Itzpapalotl saw beyond the battle, for she knew that even if Cipactli was defeated, which she was sure it would be, there was the other matter to deal with: the Chaos Spawn. Cipactli was only one half of destruction, and for all its power, the Chaos Spawn posed an equal threat. They might have been scattered, but they were certainly an issue.

If they killed Cipactli now, without preparing for its fragments, those pieces would find new ways to grow. New ways to hunger. Itzpapalotl knew this, and so she turned her attention not to Cipactli, but to the problems not yet seen.

She flew to the farthest corners of the cosmos, taking Ometecuhtli and Omecihuatl with her, and found the Primordial of Life. At her request, the Primordial was split into two divine beings. Itzpapalotl had a plan, but she needed help.

She needed an army.

Itzpapalotl

Pronounced: [Eets-pah-PAH-lohtl]

Meaning: Obsidian Butterfly

Goddess of: War, Strategy, Sacrifice, and Night

Appearance: Depicted with butterfly wings edged in obsidian blades and skeletal features. Her beauty is haunting and terrible, often shown with sharp claws or jaguar markings.

Fun Fact: Though often feared, Itzpapalotl was not purely destructive. In some traditions, she guarded paradise and the souls of children who died young, showing her duality as both fierce protector and ruthless warrior.

History: One of the Tzitzimime, celestial beings associated with stars and chaos, Itzpapalotl was the Goddess of War and understood the cost of every battle. She was not a brute force, but a tactician. Her rituals often involved the flaying of skin and symbolic transformation, marking her as a god who understood that strength came from pain, and clarity from suffering.

CHAPTER 5
THE GODS OF LIFE

With so much destruction and so much death, one might forget that, even in times of war and times of loss, there is always hope, and there is always life. Grass may grow, and grass may die, but what the grass doesn't do is care for the biddings of others. Grass will always try to grow, no matter what. It is the spirit of life that compels it to do so, for that is the true purpose of life: to persevere.

The Primordial of Life became the Gods of Life: Cihuacoatl and Xipe Totec. The Lady of Snakes and the Flayed One. Both Gods of Life held the importance of life above all else, and in that life a cycle must be upheld: Life, Death, Rebirth. They both agreed suffering was necessary, that sacrifices had to be made, yet how those sacrifices came about was where the two disagreed.

Cihuacoatl believed that suffering began with life, while Xipe Totec believed suffering came with the end of life. Their arguments were as follows:

Cihuacoatl believed that the creation of life was the
most difficult part of life, for the burden of a life giver is
immeasurable. One does not simply create and end one's
responsibility there; the creator is responsible for the life
they have created. If you create life, you must protect that
life, raise that life, care for and watch over it. You have not
just created life, you have created purpose and burden.
To create life is to accept all of the responsibilities that will
come with being that life's creator. Then, once that life is
created, you are the life's guidance, forever, even after
you die. For your guidance will be their guidance, and
so and so forth, until the end of all time. This is a suffering
that has no equal, and that suffering is what makes life so
precious and beautiful.

Xipe Totec believed that end of life was the most difficult
part of life, for to live a life and be born is easy, but to face
its end is an impossibility. All one has known their whole
life is life, and all they have known while they live is to live.
A life, and living that life, is the most incredible thing you
will ever do. To accept the end of your life is a maddening
thought, for it is an acceptance to the end of all you've
ever known. To die is to look back at your life, all you
have ever known, and wonder. Wonder what could have
been, and wonder at what could still be. When you face
the end of your life, assuming death does not take you
too early, you will be left with a million questions and the
knowledge that you will never receive the answers. That is
true suffering, and that is why life is so beautiful.

Cihuacoatl and Xipe Totec were two halves of the same whole:
to live is to suffer, and to suffer is to live. But suffering doesn't

always have to be a bad thing; in fact, lots of great things come from suffering. To plant corn, one must destroy what was there before. To give birth is to suffer, so that new life may begin. To raise kids, to grow crops, to protect life, and to take life. All of these things required suffering, and all of these things made life special.

As for Itzpapalotl, she had a decision to make: Where would her suffering begin? At the start of life, or at its end? Would she suffer so that her army might not? Or would she pass on the burden of suffering to those she created? Her decision took time, but after much thought, she realized what she had to do: she would choose both. She would choose to be a mother. She would choose suffering, from beginning to end, for all eternity. To become a mother is suffering, and it is joy. It is suffering that never ends, and it is joy that always lasts.

To create life was pleasure, but to grow life was pain. To give life was suffering, but to raise life was a joy. Pleasure and Pain. Suffering and Joy. A burden for all mothers, for all of time. And to all mothers, Itzpapalotl made a promise: she would protect them from harm, and when death arrived for a mother or for her children, Itzpapalotl would personally guide them to the great beyond.

Cihuacoatl

Pronounced: [See-wah-KOH-ahtl]

Meaning: Snake Woman

God of: Childbirth, Pain, Protection, Motherhood, and the Threshold Between Life and Death

Appearance: Often depicted as a fierce woman carrying a shield and a weapon, sometimes with a serpent headdress or skull motifs. Her face is sometimes skeletal, symbolizing her connection to death and rebirth.

Fun Fact: In Aztec mythology, Cihuacoatl was also the title given to the highest priest or deputy ruler in Tenochtitlan, often acting as co-ruler alongside the emperor. This shows the power and reverence tied to her name.

History: Cihuacoatl is a complex and ancient goddess who represents both the pain of birth and the struggle of death. She was believed to appear at crossroads, crying for her lost child, an omen for mothers and warriors alike. As a patron of midwives and those who died in childbirth, she straddled the border between life and death. Her temples were places of both mourning and honor, especially for fallen women, who were seen as warriors equal to those who died in battle.

Xipe Totec

Pronounced: [Shee-peh TOH-tek]

Meaning: Our Lord the Flayed One

God of: Rebirth, Agriculture, Renewal, Pain, and Transformation

Appearance: Depicted wearing the flayed skin of a human corpse over his own body, often with one hand pulling back the loose skin to reveal the vibrant red body beneath.

Fun Fact: Xipe Totec's rituals were among the most intense in Mesoamerica. Flayed human skins were worn by priests to symbolize the renewal of crops, just as the Earth sheds its old skin to give birth to a new harvest.

History: Xipe Totec is a god of paradox, his image horrifying, his purpose vital. He represents the painful transformation necessary for growth. His worship included gladiatorial combat, offerings, and ritual flaying during the festival Tlacaxipehualiztli. Far from a god of cruelty, Xipe Totec reminded his followers that beauty is born through struggle. He brought fertility to the land and hope to the future by embracing decay as a necessary part of creation.

CHAPTER 6
THE STAR DEMONS

From the womb of Itzpapalotl came the Tzitzimime, the Star Demons.

The Tzitzimime were monstrous beings of pure contradiction: grotesque yet beautiful, ferocious yet protective. They were feminine in appearance, with the curves of a beautiful woman, and long black hair. The rest of their appearance was something out of a nightmare, for as they were women, they were also beings of destruction.

Armed, Itzpapalotl led her daughters to war. Across the shattered universe, the Star Demons spread like a second extinction, hunting those who came before them. The Chaos Spawn made the paths, and the Star Demons followed. Where the Chaos went, the Star Demons followed, and when they found the spawn of creeping crawling Chaos, they were destroyed without mercy or hesitation.

The onslaught was so relentless, it came to a point where the other gods had to step in. These Star Demons, who had only just been born, were becoming accustomed to the destruction they caused. If destruction is all one knows, then that is all that one shall do. A warning from the other gods, ignored in full.

Itzpapalotl's mission was singular and simple: destroy all the Chaos Spawn. She would not stop and she would not falter until her mission was completed. If this meant her children would be agents of destruction, so would they be. Some gods, however, would not accept being told no.

It was then that Ometecuhtli and Omecihuatl brought into being the only gods who could, in their eyes, stop the Star Demons. They created the Gods of Magic, and with them, an end to the Star Demons.

The Gods of Magic, for varying reasons, decided that being told no by Itzpapalotl was unacceptable. With the majority of the Chaos Demons defeated, the few that remained could serve a purpose. They could serve the gods.

As for the God of Magic, his view was simple: the Chaos Spawn were weapons, and in his hand, those weapons could prove useful for whatever may come.

For the Goddess of Magic, her view came from pity. The Chaos Spawn were not evil; they were acting within their nature. She was at first keen to ignore them, but when they begged for help, and begged for forgiveness, she could not stand idly by.

Together, the two Gods of Magic acted precisely, singularly in their power, and crafted a solution. They tethered the Star Demons to the sun, making it a prison. There on the sun, the Star Demons would slumber, not dead, and not a threat. Itzpapalotl was furious at this decision, but with Cipactli still a threat, and the majority of the Chaos Spawn defeated, she understood that now was not the time to fight. Now was the time to end this war, and end the war they did.

Tzitzimimeh

Pronounced: [Tsee-tsee-MEE-meh]

Meaning: Those Who Descend, or Star Demons

Role: Celestial spirits of destruction, associated with death, drought, and the end of eras

Appearance: Usually depicted as skeletal women wearing star or bone-patterned skirts, with clawed hands and exposed ribs, and sometimes holding skulls or shields. Often shown with monstrous or terrifying features, such as wide mouths or vacant eyes.

Fun Fact: The Tzitzimimeh were feared most during solar eclipses, when they were believed to descend to devour the world if the sun failed to rise again. During this time, not even the gods would descend onto the Earth.

History: The Tzitzimimeh were female deities or spirits associated with stars, especially the stars visible during the day when the sun was absent. They were believed to reside in the heavens, but would descend to Earth during cosmic instability, particularly during solar eclipses, droughts, or the destruction of a sun. In some accounts, they were considered the sisters or servants of the goddess Itzpapalotl, and in others, they were seen as ancient, chaotic forces opposed to cosmic order.

CHAPTER 7
THE GODS OF MAGIC

The tide of the war had turned, and it was nearing its end. With the Chaos Spawn defeated and under control, and with Cipactli wounded and bound, the final battle had finally come. The gods would finally defeat Cipactli, and who would lead them? The Gods of Magic: Tezcatlipoca and Tlazolteotl, the Smoking Mirror and the Filth Goddess.

Tezcatlipoca was born holding an obsidian mirror: flawless, black, and alive. It showed not just reflections, but truths: the future and the past, desire and failure. All magic known and unknown lived in that mirror. And Tezcatlipoca did not simply gaze into it, he commanded it.

Tezcatlipoca became the God of Magic, and with this magic he created many great and powerful things. He conjured into the mirror powerful spells that only he knew. He learned how to conjure monsters and demons, and even learned how to change his own shape. Tezcatlipoca created a hundred forms, each with their own names and their own powers.

He created powerful weapons like the Rod of True Sight, a staff that could see the true intentions of anyone. For the specific purpose of defeating Cipactli, he created a dagger called Night Sky That Cuts the Wind, and this dagger removed immortality from anyone and anything. He stabbed this dagger into Cipactli's flesh, and as he did, its many mouths screamed, and yelled, begging for the pain to stop.

Everyone learned in that moment the kind of man Tezcatlipoca was, and the kind of man he wasn't. He was not a man of mercy, he was a man of action. He was not a man who would show kindness to his enemy, he would strike without warning. He would not stop when he needed to, he would stop when he wanted to.

Tezcatlipoca was nearly as cruel as one could be, and with his great power, the others feared him and what he could do. For Tezcatlipoca held two of the most dangerous things one could have: greatness and potential. It was one thing to be great, and one thing to have great potential, but to be great and still hold potential? Such a thing is saved for only those who come once in a lifetime.

Tezcatlipoca, as you will come to find, was not a kind man. One day he would be. One day far away. But for now, and for a great long while, he was cruel. Only in rare moments, such as this, was his cruelty ever answered.

In the moment of piercing the body of Cipactli, and having no emotions toward the screaming of the Chaos, one of the mouths of Cipactli lashed out and bit off the leg of

Tezcatlipoca. Tezcatlipoca screamed in agony, the first god to ever experience true pain and mutilation.

Everything from the knee down was gone, and it would never return. No matter what the gods would do, or what magic he possessed, or what the Gods of Life and medicine tried, his leg would never return.

In its place, he took his mirror and formed it into a leg, and he did this for two reasons: The first was that he did not want the others to see him as anything less than whole. He had an image to uphold, and would not let that image be tarnished. The second reason was a secret to all the gods, and that secret was that when the Chaos bit into Tezcatlipoca, it infected him. The corrupting, writhing, crawling Chaos bled its way into his flesh and into his soul.

Some say that Tezcatlipoca was not cruel, or at least not as cruel as he soon came to be, and it was only this hidden curse that turned him this way. Others believe the curse only enhanced the darkness that was already in his heart.

Tezcatlipoca

Pronounced: [Tez-cah-tlee-poh-kah]

Meaning: Smoking Mirror

God of: Sorcery, Night, the North, Jaguars, Obsidian, Power, Fate, and Kings

Appearance: Tezcatlipoca is often depicted as a powerful figure with a missing foot replaced by a smoking mirror, serpent, or bone. His face is painted with black and yellow stripes; the black represents the night and death, while yellow represents power and nobility.

Fun Fact: His name, the Smoking Mirror, does not mean a mirror that has smoke emanating from it. The Smoking Mirror was a reference to obsidian, which is reflective, but not perfectly reflective. If you've ever looked into obsidian, you'll notice it has a strange effect on reflections, creating a warbly smokey sort of effect. While some have depicted him as having smoke coming from his mirror or body, this is a misunderstanding of what his name truly means.

History: One of the most ancient and powerful deities in Mesoamerica, Tezcatlipoca was worshipped long before the rise of the Aztec. He was often associated with the night sky, divine rulership, and the force of destiny. His name appears in Toltec stories and other Mesoamerican traditions, where he is shown as a bringer of conflict but also of transformation. Obsidian, sacred to Tezcatlipoca, was not just a material but a window into the spirit world. His temples stood tall, especially in Tenochtitlan, where he was honored with elaborate festivals and impersonators who would become his earthly form for a year before being sacrificed.

Tlazolteotl did not arrive with mirrors or weapons, for she needed neither. Tezcatlipoca could scheme and conjure, but her power, which was just as strong as Tezcatlipoca's, came from the magic of the soul. Her magic was to twist and bend the magic of sin.

Where Tezcatlipoca held the mirror, Tlazolteotl held the heart. She did not command magic, she seduced it and made it change for her. Where she walked, longing followed, for her beauty was unmatched, and all those who saw her, even magic, wanted her.

Where she stood, secrets spilled, begging to be heard by her. Tlazolteotl became the Goddess of Sin, but also the Goddess of Purification. For every shameful act, she offered forgiveness. But she never gave anything for free, and nothing ever came easy.

First, you had to admit your sin, of your own free will. She would not tear these secrets from you, nor would she demand your truth. You offered and she accepted, for true forgiveness comes only when you are willing to accept change.

Tlazolteotl created no spells, no staffs, and no blades. Her power came from empathy, and offering an ear to listen and a mouth to speak advice. From these sins, and from these truths, her power would grow, and change would occur. If you had the strength, but needed more, she would be there to offer it. She was a guide and a guardian of truth.

But do not think she was entirely good, for just as she forgave, she tempted as well. She was the Goddess of Pleasure and abundance and offered you anything you wanted, if you chose it. Pleasures of the body, mind, and spirit were given, without price. Tlazolteotl even offered her own body to both gods and mortals, if they so chose. Few could say no, for Tlazoteotl had no equal in looks, and often she wore few to no clothes at all.

She forgave, she tempted, and she punished. Yes, she would tempt, and yes, if asked, she would give, but do not think partaking in the pleasures of a goddess came without a price. To those who gave in to pleasures of the body, sores and sicknesses and filth would cover you until you sought forgiveness.

On those who lied and tricked, she forced confession, not just to her, but to all. She demanded confession, and while not all might know one's lies, all would know one's forgiveness. If you chose to keep your lies, Tlazolteotl would keep your soul, refusing to let you leave into the great beyond.

Absolution was offered, but never endlessly. In fact, it was offered once. Only once. For smaller misdeeds and sins, forgiveness was easy. But for great acts? Betrayals of love, acts of murder, disregard for community? Those acts could be forgiven only once, and never more. Should acts such as those be committed twice, the sinner's soul was hers, for all eternity.

Her weapons were truth and guilt, and even among the gods, this power was formidable. Even against Cipactli, this power was useful.

While others sought to stab and fight Cipactli, Tlazolteotl stepped forward, no weapon in hand. She did not sneak up to Cipactli; she approached it head-on, and with the softest of touches, she kissed Cipactli and offered forgiveness.

Tlazolteotl understood what the others could not: Cipactli was not evil, it was acting within its design, just as they all used to. It had only become Chaos because the universe demanded

Chapter 7: The Gods of Magic

balance, and it had no choice but to obey. Creation gave it hunger, so it hungered, endlessly, because it *had* to. The universe gave it hunger, so it ate. And when they called it a monster, it became one.

There, on the skin of its snout, rough and trembling, she placed her lips and whispered that, should it choose to speak its mind, she would listen. And for the first time in all creation, Cipactli stopped eating. Its many mouths fell still and its claws did not strike. From somewhere deep inside its writhing mass, something quiet rose. Not peace. Not love. But guilt.

Cipactli could not understand it, and perhaps didn't want to, but the feeling was there now. Tlazolteotl felt it rise like fire, thick and choking and overwhelming. She knew, in that moment, Cipactli felt regret for its actions.

Cipactli could not change what it was, for it would always hunger, but it thought of a life for itself where the hunger could be put to rest, and instead of eating carelessly, it could eat with intention. But this thought was fleeting, and when it comes to matters of the heart, even for gods, forgiving oneself for what one has done isn't easy. Cipactli found its guilt, and that guilt bubbled to the surface, and then Cipactli ate that guilt, and buried it back down deep inside. One day it would forgive itself, but that day, and that moment, was not now.

Distracted with its own moral questions, Cipactli let down its guard just long enough for all the other gods to strike. Ometecuhtli and Omecihuatl led their forces of gods; some of which you know about, and others you do not. These gods fought together, and all at once struck down the terrible creeping crawling Chaos.

Cipactli was finally killed.

It then came time for a decision to be made. What would be done with Cipactli's body? Many ideas were noted, but finally an agreement was reached. Cipactli's body would be formed into a planet, and it would be on that planet that the gods would find their home. They would build a great world above the planet, and call it the Heavens. And below the planet, a hidden realm of Death. The surface of the planet, monsters and mortals would call home.

The gods believed that was Cipactli was dead, but the truth was kept secret. It was a secret only Tlazolteotl and two others knew of. It was true that Cipactli's body was made into the planet, but her soul? Someone had taken that and hidden it away.

Tlazolteotl saw potential in Cipactli, and felt, given enough time, she could change. She believed the crawling Chaos with endless mouths and endless hunger could be a force for good, if only given time and patience. She knew none would understand this, and so she took Cipactli's soul and gave it to the only two other gods who would understand.

The Gods of Death.

Tlazolteotl

Pronounced: [Tlah-zol-TEH-ohtl]

Meaning: Filth God

Goddess of: Sin, Confession, Lust, Cleansing, and Purification

Appearance: Often shown with a black mouth or with blackened lips and hands, symbolizing her power to consume sin. She may also appear with a broom, used to sweep away impurities, or seated atop a *temazcal* (sweat lodge).

Fun Fact: The Mesoamericans were the first known civilization in the world to invent and regularly use steam baths, called *temazcales*, for spiritual and physical purification. These sweat lodges were directly tied to Tlazolteotl's worship, where people confessed sins and expelled guilt through heat, sweat, and ritual cleansing.

History: Tlazolteotl is one of the most complex goddesses in the Aztec pantheon, embodying both the cause of moral transgression and its remedy. She encouraged lust and wrongdoing, but also offered purification through confession. Her role was deeply tied to ritual acts of cleansing, especially those done in the *temazcal*, and she was often invoked before death to absolve final sins. The guilty would sweat, confess, and be purified by her sacred rites, emerging physically clean and spiritually whole. Despite her association with sin, she was revered not as a corrupter but as a redeemer.

CHAPTER 8
THE GODS OF DEATH

The God of Death was Mictlantecuhtli, and his wife, the Goddess of Death, was named Mictecacihuatl. He was the Lord of Mictlan, and she was the Lady of the Dead. He ruled over the land, and she ruled over the people. The first soul to come to their land of the dead was Cipactli, and she would prove to be their greatest challenge, and greatest accomplishment.

When Cipactli was defeated, her soul was dragged down to Mictlan, the underworld of both gods and mortals. Cipactli's soul, however, was proving to be just as strong as her body, and while the intention was to help her overcome her tenacious hunger, to do so would not be easy. Mictlantecuhtli and Mictecacihuatl created a series of obstacles that would weaken her soul enough to be cured. These were called the Nine Trials of Mictlan.

Trial One: The River of Blood

Upon arriving in Mictlan, you are met with a river of blood that you must cross. The river is dangerous and fast, and can carry you far away from where you need to go. Cipactli stepped into the river, and she was carried away. Bits of her soul fell into the river until she eventually crawled out on the other side, though a whole year had passed.

Trial Two: The Place Where the Mountains Crash Together

You must travel along a path, and on that path, on either side of you, are two jagged cliffs that eternally sway back and forth, crashing against one another at random. The purer your soul, the slower they crash. For Cipactli, who had caused so much chaos, the mountains crushed and crashed until her soul was worn.

Trial Three: The Obsidian Mountain

Here, obsidian spikes jut in every direction and razor edges line every surface. You must climb this mountain of razor blades, for failing or dying will return you to the bottom of the mountain. It took Cipactli several years to climb this mountain, and when she did, she was much smaller than when she had started.

Trial Four: Place of the Wind That Cuts like Knives

The fourth trial sees you survive a wind storm unlike anything you've ever seen. In the wind are blades, not of physical harm, but of emotional distress. For every blade that cuts you, your mind wanes. Memories bleed from you, never to return. For Cipactli, this meant that as she had neared its end, she had practically forgotten who she was and everything she had done.

Trial Five: The Place Where People Fly

Here, trust triumphs over common sense. A great blustering wind will throw you around, dragging you every direction you don't want to go. Eventually, you'll realize that the only way to overcome the wind is to accept it. Cipactli learned this lesson after a whole year of being thrown around.

Trial Six: The Place of Flying Arrows

Arrows are shot at you, at random, and from every direction. They have no source, but their destination is always the same. You will not die from these arrows, but you will feel pain. Cipactli felt this pain, and it became so overwhelming she was driven mad.

Trial Seven: The Place Where Hearts Are Eaten

While we'd call them jaguars, their true forms cannot be described. They are beasts of immense size, with equally immense hunger. They will claw and bite and tear out your heart. They hide in the shadows and every time you die, you must start over. For Cipactli, this journey took a whole year until she was eventually able to pass.

Trial Eight: The Monster in the Lake

Formed from her own likeness, Cipactli met a monster with many mouths and many eyes and many claws. She swam through the river, and every time it would grab her and drown her, and she'd awaken at the lake's edge. Over and over she tried, until, a year later, she had succeeded.

Trial Nine: The Judgment

Cipactli arrived at the throne room of Mictlantecuhtli and Mictecacihuatl. Her monstrous form was gone, and her mind was broken and fixed, until she was no longer a Primordial of Chaos, but a being of free thought and free will. She begged for forgiveness for what she had done. Forgiving her, Mictlantecuhtli and Mictecacihuatl tore her soul into pieces, then put her soul back together.

She would get a second chance at life, though not quite yet.

For now, the Lord and Lady of the Dead had to get their realm of the dead ready, for the Earth had been created, and there were many guests to soon welcome.

PART 2

THE AGE OF GODS

Aztec mythology gives us an abundance of stories that take place in an era of "whenever." That's to say, they don't have specific points in the mythology they anchor to. In theory, some of these stories could have happened later. However, in many of these stories, a narrative begins to form: the Tonantzin, a group of female goddesses who helped each other.

In Part 3, I have curated a collection of stories that either fit, or could fit, into this specific era: stories of Wild Gods hunting Deer Monsters, of romance and heartbreak, of Goddesses who dared not be stopped. This is the Age of Gods.

CHAPTER 9
THE THIRTEEN HEAVENS

The Thirteen Heavens were the eternal home for the gods, and their fortress where they rested and created a plan of attack. Quetzalcoatl and Huitzilopochtli had been defeated and were gone. Tezcatlipoca was wounded and fighting off madness. Tlazolteotl fled to the Earth to find the misbegotten monsters she had created. Mictlantecuhtli and Mictecacihuatl hungered for death and could no longer be trusted. Itzpapalotl had long since disappeared, and no one knew where she had gone.

Within the Thirteen Heavens, the gods found grace and peace. Each heaven was a layer, and each layer belonged to a god.

The Thirteenth Heaven, the Place of Two, was the highest, and this was the very soul of the Thirteen Heavens. This was the place of duality, the breath-place, the throne of Ometecuhtli and Omecihuatl. They sat together, always apart, always facing, always equal. Together they would be the very force that protected the Thirteen Heavens.

The Twelfth Heaven was the Place of the Gods. This would be where the future God King would rule from, where his council would live, and where all gods would leave the heavens and descend to Earth. For now, there would be no God King, nor council. Soon, however, that would change.

The Eleventh Heaven was the Region of Red. This was where the Fire Gods lived, and all of fire lived with them. Xiuhtecuhtli, the Fire Lord, ruled here.

The Tenth Heaven, the Region of Yellow, belonged to the sun, and this is where it went when it needed to rest.

The Ninth Heaven was the Region of White, and this was where the altar of Quetzalcoatl rested. His Jade Tablet sat on a pedestal, and all would remember his sacrifice. For some reason, though none knew why, the Tzitzimimitl (Star Demons) chose to stay here.

The Eighth Heaven was the Place Where the Obsidian Knives Creak, and this was the gateway to Mictlan. This heaven was freezing cold, guarded by Itztlacoliuhqui, and was also the home for Itzpapalotl, should she ever return.

The Seventh Heaven was the Region of Blue, and this was the dedicated altar to Huitzilopochtli and a remembrance of his sacrifice.

The Sixth Heaven was the Dark Green Space, and this was where Tezcatlipoca called home. This place was always dark and always night. This is the place the Lords of the Night called home.

The Fifth Heaven was the Sinking Sky. During the day, all of the stars in the sky rested here. At night, they would rush from this home and cover the blanket of space above the Earth.

The Fourth Heaven was the Big Star, and as of now, this heaven was empty.

The Third Heaven was Where the Sun Moves, and as of now, this heaven was empty.

The Second Heaven was Where the Stars Move, and this was where all the Gods of Space lived.

The First Heaven was Where the Moon Moves, and this was where the Moon rested. The first heaven was the lowest heaven, and this was where many gods, especially lesser gods, lived. One such god was the God of Storms, Tlaloc.

While seen by many as a lesser god, Tlaloc had high ambitions. Tlaloc swore to himself that one day he would rise up to the highest level of the Thirteen Heavens and become the God King. Until then, however, he had a job to do. Offering himself as tribute, Tlaloc became the caretaker of the Thirteen Heavens.

Tlaloc

Pronounced: [TLAH-lock]

Meaning: He Who Makes Things Sprout

God of: Rain, Storms, Fertility, and Mountains

Appearance: Often depicted with goggle eyes, large fangs, and a mask-like face. He is shown with lightning bolts, water vessels, and sometimes frog or serpent imagery.

Fun Fact: Children were often sacrificed to Tlaloc, especially at Mount Tlaloc, and their tears were considered sacred omens of coming rain.

History: Tlaloc was one of the most powerful and widely worshipped gods in central Mexico, responsible for rain, fertility, and agricultural abundance. He ruled over Tlalocan, a lush, paradisiacal afterlife reserved for those who died by drowning, lightning, or water-related illnesses. Tlaloc controlled storms and lightning and could bring both life-giving rains and devastating floods. His worship involved offerings, ceremonies on mountaintops, and rituals to ensure seasonal rains, including child sacrifice. As a central figure in the Aztec calendar and mythos, he was one of the deities who helped govern the world during previous Suns. He is often paired or contrasted with Chalchiuhtlicue, the goddess of lakes and streams.

CHAPTER 10

LOVE, DEATH, AND MAGIC

As the caretaker of the Thirteen Heavens, Tlaloc was in charge of its daily schedules, as well its protection. To achieve this mission, Tlaloc created the Tlaloque: Tiny Storm Children.

These little storm children rode around on clouds, patrolled the heavens, and informed Tlaloc of everything there was to know. He spied on those he didn't trust, and spied on those he did, just to be certain. Tlaloc was smart about this, and nobody was the wiser to his schemes, except for Tezcatlipoca. And Tezcatlipoca? He did not like being spied on. In fact, he was so upset by this that he set out to get his revenge the only way he knew how: by crossing a line that should not be crossed.

Tlaloc, for all his merits and titles and glories, held onto one thing more than anything else: his love for his sister. Her name was Chalchiuhtlicue, and she was the goddess of waters, rivers, and oceans. She was kind, trusting, and one of the most beautiful goddesses in all the pantheon.

For no other reason than to upset Tlaloc, Tezcatlipoca made a move to try to win the heart of Chalchiuhtlicue.

Behind the back of Tlaloc, the two began to talk more and more, and eventually the two grew intimately close. However, no matter how sneaky Tezcatlipoca was, Tlaloc or his Tlaloque would interfere. They'd cause storms and rains and talk and talk about all the annoyances in their lives: anything to stop Tezcatlipoca and Chalchiuhtlicue from moving forward in their romance.

Tezcatlipoca, however, was a man of many plans and schemes, and he discovered a way to be left alone. The God of Magic and the Goddess of Rivers would race away into Mictlan, where neither Tlaloc nor the Tlaloque dared go. As it had no magic, and was quite dangerous, no one who wasn't a fool would ever go into Mictlan.

Tezcatlipoca, however, made a deal with the Lord and Lady of the Dead. He promised a favor to them if he stayed protected, and so the favor was honored. In the land of the dead, Tezcatlipoca and Chalchiuhtlicue found love.

In their secret hiding spot, Tezcatlipoca and Chalchiuhtlicue spent nearly every second of every day together. Eventually, Tlaloc learned what had happened and stormed into Mictlan, angry and loud.

Mictlantecuhtli and Mictecacihuatl, the rulers of the underworld, cared very little and mocked him for what they viewed as childish behavior.

Tlaloc was furious at the whole situation and wished to do a great many things, but he was not king, he was custodial. He wanted to banish Tezcatlipoca from the Thirteen Heavens, but couldn't. He wished to do the same to Mictlantecuhtli and Mictecacihuatl, but once again could not. A god can only command those beneath his level. As Tlaloc was on the lowest level, he had no sway over anyone...except his sister. He banished her to Earth, and swore she could never return. It was a bad decision, and a dangerous one as well. Earth was filled with monsters, and had she gone to Earth alone, perhaps she might have died.

Chalchiuhtlicue, however, was not alone. She had the Tonantzin on her side.

Chalchiuhtlicue

Pronounced: [Chal-chee-oo-TLEE-kweh]

Meaning: She of the Jade Skirt

Goddess of: Lakes, Streams, Birth, and Cleansing

Appearance: Depicted wearing a skirt of jade or turquoise ribbons, with water flowing from her garments. Often shown with a headdress and earspools, she is associated with rivers, waterfalls, and amniotic waters.

Fun Fact: In Aztec belief, she ruled the Fourth Sun, which ended in a great flood that transformed humans into fish.

History: Chalchiuhtlicue was revered as the goddess of fresh water, fertility, and childbirth, responsible for lakes, rivers, and springs. She was also a protector of midwives and newborns. Often seen as the consort or female counterpart to Tlaloc, she balanced his destructive storms with nourishing and purifying waters. Her domain included both the life-giving force of water and its potential for overwhelming destruction. In Aztec myth, she ruled over the Fourth Age of the world before it ended in a catastrophic flood. Worship of Chalchiuhtlicue was widespread, especially in rituals involving purification, baptism-like ceremonies, and river offerings.

CHAPTER 11
THE TONANTZIN

There were rules in the Heavens. Even for gods.

When Chalchiuhtlicue broke the rules and wishes of her brother, there was nothing anyone could do. She had loved her brother, had always trusted him—in return, he cast her out in rage and banished her from the Thirteen Heavens.

By her side she expected Tezcatlipoca to join her, but he did not. He would visit her, and promised to keep her in his heart, but he refused to leave the Thirteen Heavens.

As she stood on the Earth, alone, she cried. Soon, the Earth was covered in oceans and lakes and rivers, all from the tears of a scorned woman. A woman who, for now, saw no way nor want to ever trust men again. One could hardly blame her.

Surprisingly, Chalchiuhtlicue was soon joined by other goddesses. They decided that women, mothers, and daughters needed to be protected. If they did not protect them, who would? Chalchiuhtlicue stood as proof that not even the bond of family mattered to some men.

The goddesses became sisters by vow, not by blood. They called themselves the Tonantzin: the Many Mothers, and announced that they were the Protectors of All Women.

Each one held power, and together, the goddesses did what the gods could not. They put aside their differences, gave each other a voice, and together they stood as a single powerful threat.

There were many within the Tonantzin, but a few names echoed louder than others:

Cihuacoatl, the Snake Woman, Goddess of Mothers and Birth, led the group. She carried a knife in one hand and a baby in the other. She guarded every mother, even those not yet pregnant.

Itzpapalotl, the Goddess of War, was Cihuacoatl's sword and shield. She was the fury and anger of the Tonantzin, and personally saw to it that every man—be he god or mortal—would suffer her wrath.

Tlazolteotl, the Eater of Filth, watched over women who had been wronged and created monsters and curses to chase after the men who had committed these wrongs.

And now Chalchiuhtlicue, Goddess of Rivers and Lakes, found herself among them. Together, the Tonantzin built a sanctuary and did so in the eye of all, a threat to those who dared get in their way. They refused to hide, and demanded respect.

Cihuacoatl, the first mother, soon discovered that not all castles are free from threats. Chaos Monsters still roamed the lands, hiding in the Earth's wounds. They smelled the coming life and hungered for it, and when Cihuacoatl went on a walk with her baby one day, they struck.

Cihuacoatl called out for help, but none came. She was too far from the sanctuary. Too alone. As the monster closed in, Cihuacoatl turned and faced it, and prepared to fight.

Tonantzin

Pronounced: [Toh-nahn-tzeen]

Meaning: Our Revered Mother

Goddess of: Motherhood, Earth, Creation, and Death

Appearance: Tonantzin is not depicted as a single figure, but as a divine title held by powerful mother goddesses such as Coatlicue, Cihuacoatl, Toci, and others. Common visual themes include serpent skirts, skulls, clawed feet, and symbols of both life and decay.

Fun Fact: After the Spanish conquest, Indigenous people continued to call the Virgin of Guadalupe *Tonantzin*, linking her to earlier mother goddesses and demonstrating how sacred titles can carry across religious shifts.

History: In Nahua tradition, *Tonantzin* was a revered title given to the great goddesses who embodied motherhood, the

Earth, and the life-death cycle. It was not the name of a single goddess, but a way to honor figures like Coatlicue (Mother of the Gods), Cihuacoatl (Goddess of Birth and Warfare), and Toci (Grandmother of the People). These goddesses were seen as nurturing and terrifying, creators and destroyers, life-givers and devourers. Their power shaped the land and its people, and their temples often stood on mountains, representing sacred wombs of the Earth.

CHAPTER 12

THE WEEPING WOMAN

The monsters never stood a chance.

How could they survive the wrath of a mother fighting for her child? There was no force in this world, or any other, that could stop a mother's fury. Yet, it was this fury that would come to be Cihuacoatl's greatest regret.

Somehow, some way, in the middle of the fight, Cihuacoatl's baby went missing. Was he stolen? Did he crawl away? Did he get eaten when she wasn't looking? She had no idea. All she knew was that, even though she fought with all her might, her baby was gone.

That night, the jungle heard the first cry of the Weeping Woman.

They say Cihuacoatl wandered for days, weeks, even months, searching rivers and caves and wind-carved stone for her son. Even the gods didn't know if he had truly died, or simply vanished. Some whispered that the Earth had swallowed him to keep him safe. Others claimed that the Chaos had stolen his soul. Cihuacoatl refused to believe either. She believed only in grief. And grief changed her.

Her skin grew pale. Her eyes, once golden, turned hollow. She stopped speaking. Stopped screaming. Only the sound of her weeping remained. She became a monster, attacking even the other gods and goddesses. She roamed the land, attacking anyone and anything she saw. Her pain was immeasurable, and so she sought to make others feel it.

Knowing that this pain would never go away, the Tonantzin came to her with a solution.

Itzpapalotl fought the Weeping Woman into submission.

Tlazolteotl ripped out the Weeping Woman, separating her from Cihuacoatl.

Chalchiuhtlicue then bound the Weeping Woman soul to the river.

Mayahuel then healed the body of Cihuacoatl.

From then on, the Weeping Woman would haunt the world, bound to the river, and endlessly sad. The Tonantzin would never speak her name again, but they remembered. To honor her, they made a vow:

No woman would ever wander alone again. No mother would ever bury her child alone. And no grief, no matter how heavy, would ever be carried by one soul alone.

This is why the Tonantzin are feared by some, worshipped by others, but respected by all. They are not gods of war or judgment. They are not the rulers of the skies or the underworld. They are unity bound by love and pain.

As for what happened to the baby? He was alive and he became...the Wild God.

La Llorona

Pronounced: [Lah Yoh-roh-nah]

Meaning: The Weeping Woman

Spirit of: Grief, Guilt, Lost Children, and Wandering Souls

Appearance: A ghostly woman dressed in white, often with long black hair obscuring her face. She is usually seen near rivers or lakes, crying for her lost children. Sometimes her face is beautiful, other times skeletal.

Fun Fact: The story of La Llorona is one of the oldest folktales in the Americas, with roots in Aztec mythology. Some versions connect her to the goddess Cihuacoatl, who was said to cry out in the night, warning of tragedy.

History: La Llorona is a legendary spirit who wanders the Earth weeping for her drowned children. The most common version tells of a woman who, in a moment of madness or vengeance, drowns her children and is cursed to search for them forever. Her story blends Spanish colonial influence with older Indigenous beliefs, particularly those surrounding women who die in childbirth or goddesses of mourning like Cihuacoatl. In pre-Hispanic times, tales were told of a woman crying at night, foretelling doom, and this figure merged with post-conquest Catholic themes of sin, punishment, and repentance. Today, La Llorona is both a warning and a symbol of sorrow, appearing in stories, songs, and nightmares throughout Latin America.

CHAPTER 13

THE WILD GOD HUNTS THE DEER WOMAN

What Cihuacoatl would never figure out was that during her battle, her baby fell from her satchel and was saved by the woodland animals who cowered and hid nearby.

Mixcoatl was raised in the forest by several animals, and each animal taught him all that they knew. Not just how to survive, but how to live as one with the forest.

The jaguar taught him to move without sound, to strike from the shadows and vanish like smoke.

The snake taught him patience, that the strongest strike is the one that waits for the right opportunity.

The rabbit taught him how to fight, to hold no fear and fight with bravery.

Each lesson became a part of him, and he grew stronger and stronger every day. His weapon of choice was the bow and arrow; his arrows never missed. Not only did they not miss, the force with which they struck their prey was incredible. His arrows could split mountains and whole forests, and with a glare of his eye, he could redirect his arrow any way he wanted to.

Every animal was his friend, and he was friend to every animal. He learned the skills of the animals, their gifts, and their powers. He talked to them, and they to him, and when he was referred to by the animals he was always referred to as family.

Mixcoatl learned how to hunt, and how to survive, and in time he grew up. He was raised not as a god, but as a legend of the forest. A magical protector of animals, known to have a magical bow, with arrows that could not miss.

One day, two spirits approached Mixcoatl, seeking his help. One was named Xiuhnel (Turquoise Man) and the other was Mimich (Little Fish). Xiuhnel was made of turquoise entirely, and Mimich was entirely a fish, though he had arms and legs like a man.

They came to Mixcoatl with a simple request: There was a deer woman who was half-woman, half-deer, and more beautiful than any god or goddess they had ever seen. The spirits wanted to look upon her beauty, but she was always evasive. None could track her. None except Mixcoatl. For the challenge alone, he accepted. Together, the Wild God and the two spirits ventured into the forest. After many days and

Chapter 13: The Wild God Hunts the Deer Woman

many nights, Mixcoatl tracked and found the Deer Woman. The Deer Woman was swift, but Mixcoatl was swifter. The Deer Woman was smart, but Mixcoatl was smarter. He was a predator, the greatest predator the world had ever seen. Cornering the Deer Woman, he captured her with a rope and net, but the Deer Woman was more than met the eye.

The Deer Woman, who was once beautiful beyond compare, turned into a monster, growing two hideous and misshapen deer heads. Her arms sprouted other arms, like branches growing on branches, and her legs multiplied like a crawling bug. Her antlers turned to obsidian, and with her heads held down, she charged forward and impaled Mimich.

Mimich howled in agony for only a moment, and then his pain was gone. Xiuhnel ran to the trees, jumping as high as he could, while Mixcoatl met the Deer Woman head-on. He avoided her antlers, one by one tying up her arms and legs, and striking her with his fist so hard she fell unconscious.

As she slept, her beauty returned, and her monstrous form faded. Where he once ran away screaming, Xiuhnel couldn't help but find himself once again enamored with the Deer Woman's beauty. Heading out to get wood for a fire, Mixcoatl warned Xiuhnel that just because she was caught did not mean she was not a threat. He warned him to stay away from the Deer Woman, and if she spoke, to ignore it.

Of course, Xiuhnel failed at this simple task.

When Mixcoatl returned, he found the Deer Woman freed from her bindings. Xiuhnel, it seemed, had been seduced. A promise of a wonderful night, Mixcoatl was sure. A promise broken, for the Deer Woman stood above Xiuhnel, her hooves coated in the spirit's blood. She had trampled him to death.

Mixcoatl readied an arrow and aimed it straight for her head, offering her a single warning. If she moved, he would fire his arrow. He warned her that however quick she thought she was, he assured her that his arrows were quicker.

Before either could make a decision, the decision was made by a third. From the skies on high descended Itzpapalotl, claws flared, teeth bared, and ready to fight.

Mixcoatl

Pronounced: [Meesh-Ko-Ahtl]

Meaning: Cloud Serpent

God of: The Hunt, the Milky Way, War Bands, and Northern Tribes

Appearance: A tall warrior cloaked in red and white stripes like cloud bands, with a black mask across his eyes and a quiver of obsidian-tipped arrows on his back.

Fun Fact: Mixcoatl was the patron god of many Chichimeca and nomadic hunter tribes of northern and central Mexico. He is considered a father to several major gods, including Quetzalcoatl.

Chapter 13: The Wild God Hunts the Deer Woman

History: Mixcoatl is an ancient Mesoamerican god associated with hunting, the stars, and nomadic warriors. His name, "Cloud Serpent," links him to both the heavens and the wild Earth below. He was often invoked by war parties and hunters alike, and some myths describe him as one of the first beings to strike Cipactli. Mixcoatl is also remembered as the father of Quetzalcoatl, born through his union with the mortal or divine woman Chimalma. Stories differ on whether Mixcoatl was murdered by his brothers or rose to become a constellation, but in all versions, his legacy lives on through the warrior bloodlines and the path of stars across the night sky.

CHAPTER 14

ARROWS AND CLAWS

It began with a tremor in the branches, a hush among the creatures, and a flash of obsidian in the midday light. The jungle, so often ruled by Mixcoatl's steady hand and silent steps, felt something new slip through its leaves. Itzpapalotl arrived without fanfare, yet every vine and flower bowed as though some hidden wind bent them. Her wings shimmered like night polished to a mirror's edge, each blade catching specks of moon that danced across her armor.

Itzpapalotl came in response to the Deer Woman's cry. In every corner of the Earth, women called for help, and she listened. Now she found a stag-footed maiden bound in nets, her breath ragged and her eyes wet with fury. Not far away stood Mixcoatl, bow raised.

The Wild God judged her a monster. Nothing more, and nothing less. The arrow left his string before a single word could form from either of them.

Itzpapalotl, having never met another god who dared raise a hand against her, did not move. She assumed such a simple arrow could do her no harm, and so when she raised an arm to deflect the arrow, her scream of pain surprised none more than herself.

Painful, but no reason to retreat. Itzpapalotl advanced, closing the distance in a heartbeat, her obsidian claws slicing through the wind. Mixcoatl ducked beneath the first swipe, rolled across the dirt, and came up firing another arrow, this one nearly cutting her cheek.

Around them, the jungle watched, every animal silent, every leaf trembling.

As the battle raged, the other two continued to surprise each other. Itzpapalotl had never met a forest spirit who had moved so fast. Mixcoatl had never met a monster who could fly so quickly.

Realizing there was more to winning this battle than simply attacking, Mixcoatl fled into the forest. Itzpapalotl followed, but quickly became tangled in the vines and lost sight of Mixcoatl.

The jaguar taught him stealth, the snake taught him patience, and the hummingbird taught him how to strike quickly. Silence, patience, strike!

Mixcoatl struck down Itzpapalotl with a final devastating blow, and for any other spirit or monster that would have been enough...but this was Itzpapalotl. A roar that made animals cry shook the forest, and Itzpapalotl took off into the sky, slicing through everything and everyone nearby. Her rage was so great that in her mission to strike down Mixcoatl, her claws found another.

Before she could even realize what had happened, her fingers had already sliced off the head of the Deer Woman.

Deer Woman

Pronounced: [Deer Woo-muhn]

Meaning: Literal translation; associated with sacred femininity and the deer spirit

Spirit of: Feminine Vengeance, Wild Nature, Protection of Women

Appearance: A stunningly beautiful woman with the legs or feet of a deer. Sometimes she has antlers or glowing eyes. Her lower half always betrays her true, wild nature.

Fun Fact: In many Native American traditions, if you look down and see hooves instead of feet, you're already too late.

History: Deer Woman is a widespread spirit figure across Indigenous cultures of North America, including the Lakota, Ojibwe, Ponca, Omaha, Muscogee, and Cherokee peoples. She is both feared and respected, known to appear as a beautiful young woman who seduces men, especially those who are violent, unfaithful, or predatory.

Once alone, she reveals her hooves and either tramples them, leads them to their deaths, or causes them to waste away in obsession. Yet in other stories, she is a silent protector who watches over women and children, especially in the wilds.

Though her origins vary, Deer Woman is a symbol of justice, warning, and untamed feminine power. In modern times, she has become an icon among Indigenous artists and activists, particularly in movements supporting missing and murdered Indigenous women (MMIW), where she represents the wrath and resilience of Native women throughout history.

CHAPTER 15

THE SHIELD GODDESS

The body of the Deer Woman lay disfigured among the roots and moss, her fur matted with blood, her limbs still caught between the form of beast and woman. Her eyes were open but empty, staring skyward as if asking the stars to explain what had happened.

Itzpapalotl stood above her, breath shaking, her obsidian wings low and lifeless. She had not meant to kill. At least, not meant to kill her. But the rage, the chaos, the thrill of battle still coursed through her. She was the Goddess of War, born of violence and vengeance, but even she did not expect to feel the pain of this mistake.

The Deer Woman had cried out in fear, not aggression, and in her final breath, there had been no hatred, only pleading. The forest had fallen silent. Even the winds refused to blow. A moment of silence for the innocent.

Life may pause, but death will not, and no sooner had the body grown cold than Death rose up to claim what was theirs. From the bowls of Mictlan, Mictlantecuhtli and Mictecacihuatl rose up to claim a prize they had been wanting for quite some time. Together they took the Deer Woman's body, wrapped their skeletal fingers around her, and took her down to the afterlife...at least they would have, if Itzpapalotl had not gotten in their way.

Refusing to accept her death, Itzpapalotl demanded they leave her corpse where it was. To threaten the Lord and Lady of the Dead, however, was not smart. Even outside of Mictlan, such a threat had wide-ranging consequences.

When threats were not enough, Itzpapalotl buried her claws in the stomach of Mictlantecuhtli, ripping out his insides until they hung forward like a skirt. Quickly, the Gods of Death returned to Mictlan, swearing they would return for vengeance.

It was then that Mixcoatl made his move. Distracted, his arrows would find an easy target in Itzpapalotl. The arrow flew at incredible speed, but did not find its mark. Snatched out of the sky, Chimalma leapt into action to save her fellow Tonantzin. Her body was tough, tougher than any mountain that ever dared to touch the sky. The arrows broke against her skin and fell into many tiny pieces.

Mixcoatl fired several more arrows, and Chimalma shrugged them off like annoying flies. Mixcoatl had never met a woman as tough as her, or, as he soon found out, as strong as her. When he attempted to face Chimalma in combat, he learned for the first time in his life how painful a punch can really be.

Chapter 15: The Shield Goddess

When he awoke, Mixcoatl found himself in the temple of the Tonantzin. He would stand trial for what he had done, and if he was found guilty, death would find him swiftly.

Chimalma

Pronounced: [Chee-MAHL-mah]

Meaning: Shield Hand or Hand as Shield

Goddess of: Life, Protection, Sacred Pregnancy, and Shields

Appearance: A tall and graceful woman adorned in turquoise and serpent-patterned garments, bearing a shining round shield on one arm and a glowing mark over her womb. Her face is serene but commanding, and her presence brings peace without weakness.

Fun Fact: Chimalma was the only goddess in all of Aztec mythology to give birth to twins.

History: Chimalma's name signifies defense through compassion and inner strength, and she is often seen as a divine protector of women, mothers, and unborn children. Her image was invoked by women in childbirth and by warriors who sought to defend rather than conquer. Chimalma embodies the belief that life itself is worth protecting, even when surrounded by violence, and that true strength lies in mercy held firm.

CHAPTER 16

THE TRIAL

Bound in obsidian thread and golden chain, Mixcoatl knelt at the center of the clearing. His wild hair hung over his eyes, dirt-streaked and bloodstained. Around him stood the Tonantzin, the Sacred Mothers. They had heard the cries of the Deer Woman. They had seen the broken bodies of those who had trusted too easily. And now they stood as judge, jury, and executioners.

Mixcoatl explained who he was, and where he was from, and how he came to be in this predicament. He was a hunter, Deer Woman was an animal, and he was hunting an animal. To him, no taboo was broken, for he was an animal doing what animals do. To slay him for this is to slay all predators for doing what they do.

Of all the mothers to disagree, Mixcoatl found himself with one single ally: Chimalma. Not even Cihuacoatl, his own mother, sided with him. Though, perhaps if she had known he was her son, she would have formed a different opinion.

Chimalma, a Defender, could not see the justification for killing. One innocent had already fallen, two spirits had met their end as well, and now they sought to end another's life? She couldn't agree with it. Her opinion, however, was ignored, and it was decided death was necessary. Even if by accident, murder was murder, and the only course of action was to kill the killer.

That night, it was the intention of Chimalma to free Mixcoatl, but before she could leave the palace, a lightning bolt of incredible power struck the center. From the lightning bolt stepped Tlaloc, and from his side, black smoke grew and formed into Tezcatlipoca. At their sides, Mictlantecuhtli and Mictecacihuatl tore their way open from the Earth's floor. Finally, flashes of light, both white and black, blinded all, and from those lights stood Ometecuhtli and Omecihuatl.

Tezcatlipoca arrived to demand that Mixcoatl not be killed, for he held on his soul a prophecy. Mixcoatl would father the greatest hero the world had ever seen. To kill him would be the preemptive end of this hero god.

Tlaloc had different reasons for interfering. Tlaloc cared little for Tezcatlipoca's prophecies, but he did care for the rule of law, and reminded the Tonantzin that gods shall not kill gods.

Of course, Mictlantecuhtli and Mictecacihuatl were the informers, a bit of revenge for what Itzpapalotl had done earlier.

Chapter 16: The Trial

Despite protest from Tlaloc and Tezcatlipoca, Ometecuhtli and Omecihuatl, before passing their judgment, allowed the Tonantzin to speak in reply.

The Tonantzin laid out their issues very simply:

> Tezcatlipoca was a schemer who was not to be trusted.
>
> Tlaloc's power and his rules only extended as far as the Thirteen Heavens.
>
> Mictlantecuhtli and Mictecacihuatl, they were forced to accept, did have right over the dead, but offered that they only had access to the souls, not the bodies.
>
> Above all else, the Tonantzin were the protectors of women. None could change that.

It was for these reasons that they felt they were in the right. Omecihuatl agreed, but Ometecuhtli did not, and so, a cataclysmic decision had to be made. In that moment, the Gods of Duality realized that Duality would never work as a ruler, for one cannot be of two opposite opinions and make decisions for others. A ruler needed to be an individual.

From their hands, they raised a great power, and from the words they spoke of a solution. They decided that there needed to be a single voice. A single speaker. A Tlatoani.

Tlatoani

Pronounced: [Tlah-toh-AH-nee]

Meaning: The Speaker

Role: King, ruler, or high leader of a city-state

Appearance: Tlatoani would vary in appearance but their outfits could include: sandals made of gold, beautiful quetzal feathers on their outfit or in their hair, and earrings made of shells, gold, and jade. They would wear long capes known as *Tilmahtli*, and a turquoise crown known as the *Xiuhuitzolli*.

Fun Fact: The word *Tlatoani* comes from the Nahuatl verb *tlatoa*, meaning "to speak." Ruling through speech was seen as sacred, with words holding both political and spiritual power.

History: A Tlatoani was the supreme leader of a city-state, chosen by nobles and priests for his wisdom, lineage, and ability to govern. He commanded armies, oversaw religious ceremonies, and represented the will of the gods on Earth. His power came not only from military strength, but also from his ability to speak persuasively and maintain cosmic balance. In later centuries, the ruler of the Mexica capital of Tenochtitlan was called the Huey Tlatoani, or "Great Speaker," who held authority over a vast empire.

PART 3

THE DIVINE FLOWER WAR

While Aztec mythology tells us of the Five Suns and the rise and fall of gods, it does not explain how the gods chose their leaders or how divine power was won or lost. There is no surviving myth describing the battles between gods before humanity, or how the God King came to power.

In Part 3, we imagine what might have happened if the gods held their own Divine Flower War: a series of battles between gods. This is not a historical claim, but a respectful fictional expansion built on real Aztec culture. It is a story of gods clashing not for conquest, but for a throne that will define the First Sun.

Xōchiyāōyōtl

Pronounced: [Sho-chee-YA-oh-yotl]

Meaning: Flower War/War of Flowers

Summary: Flower Wars were nonlethal scheduled battles fought between kingdoms. These battles could host anywhere from a handful of people to a few hundred. For a set amount of time, usually until dark, the warring parties would meet in combat. When someone was defeated, they were dragged back to the opponent's side and held there.

At the end, or once everyone on one side was defeated, the two sides would barter. They would either accept that those captured would be sacrificed, or they could be sold back to their kingdoms.

The purpose of the Flower War was to keep soldiers trained, keep the powerful kingdoms in power, but avoid costly and often unnecessary wars.

Fun Fact: The goal of the Flower War was twofold. On one hand, it brought in soldiers to be sacrificed, something that meant a lot to the Aztec (Mexica) Empire. On the other hand, it was a reminder to the other kingdoms of the empire's power. This was not just a statement of their power, but a reminder to avoid all-out war. And it worked.

History: Whenever a king was elected, it was often the case that he would enter into a Flower War. If the battle was a success for the king, it meant his reign would be a success as well. If he failed, it meant his rule would fail as well. This meant all kings had to be trained in warfare, and yes, some kings did lose their Flower Wars.

CHAPTER 17
SHIELD VS. ARROWS

The rules of the Flower War were simple: two gods enter, one leaves victorious. The first gods to meet in battle were Mixcoatl and Chimalma.

Chimalma entered the ring with righteous fury. She had not forgotten the Deer Woman, nor had she forgiven the man who had hunted her. Itzpapalotl might have struck the final blow, but it was Mixcoatl who had chased her, cornered her, and loosed the arrows that had driven her to panic. Chimalma saw him as a reckless force of violence, another god who believed himself above the law, one more wild thing in a world already teetering on the edge of cruelty. While she did not want him dead as the other goddesses had, she certainly did not think he was free of guilt.

When Mixcoatl entered the battlefield, he stood with his hands open, no arrow notched, and offered no tricks. He spoke plainly. He admitted his part in what happened. He said he had made a mistake, a mistake formed in ignorance. He looked Chimalma in the eye and said he was prepared to face judgment, offering her the victory against him in this contest.

Chimalma told him no. If he truly sought redemption, she would not accept surrender. He would fight her, and the outcome would be earned, not given.

Mixcoatl nodded and raised his bow.

The battle began like thunder.

Mixcoatl's arrows were unlike any other, each one kissed by the breath of the jaguar, the strike of the serpent, the silence of the owl. They moved faster than sound, swifter than thought. Chimalma's shield danced with her, deflecting shot after shot. Sparks flew as obsidian arrowheads scraped the indestructible surface of her shield. She moved not just with power, but with purpose, matching his every move. It was not just strength or skill that made her so dangerous, it was determination. She knew who she was. She knew what she stood for. And she knew she should be the first God King.

As the fight wore on, the two began to exchange banter, acknowledging each other's skill and fighting prowess. Chimalma was strong and tough, and Mixcoatl was quick and precise. Every arrow fired was an arrow defended. It seemed, to Chimalma at least, that she simply had to wait until Mixcoatl ran out of arrows.

Then, Mixcoatl stepped back. He reached into the quiver on his back and drew an arrow unlike the others. It was made from a branch of the oldest tree in the forest, tied with the feather of the first hummingbird to ever fly, and held the fang of the sharpest tooth from the largest jaguar. It glowed softly with the forest's power, asking for its help. It answered.

Mixcoatl drew back the arrow, and fired.

It tore through the air with a howl. The gods watching from above leaned forward in awe and cheered. It was an arrow that could pierce mountains. It could split rivers. And it was aimed directly at Chimalma's heart.

She raised her shield. Not in fear. Not in panic. But in perfect, unflinching confidence. Others might have run or tried to flee or dodge, but Chimalma trusted her abilities. She held her ground, planted her feet, and met the arrow with her shield.

The arrow struck. The shield splintered. The unstoppable force met the immovable object.

In a burst of energy, Chimalma's shield exploded, and the force of it threw Chimalma back, dust and debris billowing around her like smoke. For a moment, no one could see, but everyone was sure she had been defeated.

Then the wind cleared, and there she stood, kneeling, breathing heavily, but alive. Her shield was cracked, her arm trembling, but she had not fallen. Her feet were firm. Her eyes locked on Mixcoatl.

She rose, stepped forward, and struck him once in the chest with the flat of her hand. It was not a violent blow. It did not break bones or draw blood. But it was enough.

Mixcoatl dropped to his knees, exhausted, smiling even as he collapsed onto the floor.

Chimalma was declared the victor.

Tlipotl

Pronounced: [Teel-pohtl]

Meaning: Dart (Bow and Arrow)

Used by: Hunters, warriors, and gods such as Mixcoatl

Appearance: Longbows carved from ash or mesquite, often decorated with feathers and painted glyphs. Arrows tipped in obsidian or flint, fletched with eagle or hummingbird feathers.

Fun Fact: Arrows were sometimes ritually "breathed upon" to bless them before battle.

History: The bow and arrow were sacred tools of survival and sacrifice. Hunters used them to feed their people, and warriors used them to defend their cities and wage Flower Wars. In myth, gods like Mixcoatl wielded divine bows that shot arrows faster than sound, each carrying the spirit of a jungle animal. Arrows were not simply weapons, they were messages sent by the will of their user. The bow represented vision and distance, while the arrow symbolized choice and consequence. Among the stars, constellations were often interpreted as great bows stretching across the sky, aiming at the hearts of fate.

Chimalli

Pronounced: [Chee-Mall-e]

Meaning: Shield

Used by: Elite warriors, eagle and jaguar knights, and goddesses such as Chimalma

Appearance: Circular, often made from woven reeds or leather stretched over a wooden frame, covered in fur, feathers, and patterned fabrics. Sometimes reinforced with obsidian shards or metallic rings.

Fun Fact: A warrior's shield was more than defense, it was identity. Each shield carried a family crest, godly emblem, or animal spirit, linking the bearer to divine protection. No two shields were the same.

History: Shields in Aztec culture were symbols of both protection and prestige. A well-made *chimalli* could block arrows, spears, or even magic, and was often used with a short weapon like a *macuahuitl* or club. In mythology, Chimalma, the mother shield, was said to defend those who could not defend themselves. Shields were not passive tools. They moved with their bearers, danced in ritual combat, and pulsed with ancestral power. Breaking a shield was a great dishonor. Holding the line with one was a mark of divine favor.

CHAPTER 18
STORM VS. DEATH

There were few gods more respected than Mictlantecuhtli. He did not command with fire or thunder. He did not demand offerings with force or trickery. He ruled by silence and stature, and in his domain, the only certainty was that he was above all others.

Tlaloc was right to fear him, for who was Tlaloc to Mictlantecuhtli? Tlaloc was a guardian at best, certainly nothing near a king of the dead. He commanded storms, though he could hardly control them. Well, he could control them just as well as he could control his emotions.

Tlaloc entered the battle with a certainty that he would lose. Fighting was never his passion nor his skill, and he half-intended to fight just enough to put on a show, then quit gracefully. Yet, as with all great men, a powerful woman stood behind him.

Chalchiuhtlicue approached her brother before the battle and reminded him that Mictlantecuhtli was only strong in his world.

A world he was not currently in. She reminded her brother that storms are unmatched in power, and should he simply focus that strength, he would be strong enough to win his battle.

She reminded her brother that his goal was to rise in rank, and in this moment, he could do that. To have faith in himself was all he had to do, and though his sister owed him no grace, she offered it to him. She forgave him, encouraged him, and reminded him of his destiny to be greater than what he was given.

Tlaloc attacked first, summoning a bolt of lightning and striking down Mictlantecuhtli.

The laughter from his bony dead body echoed throughout the field, making all save his wife uncomfortable. Pain was nothing to a rotting corpse, and a lightning bolt was only that: pain. Temporary, fleeting, pain.

Over and over, Mictlantecuhtli was struck with lightning, hail, and rain. Over and over, the Lord of the Dead laughed. Strolling forward, Mictlantecuhtli took his time, having not a single doubt that he would win this battle.

With each lightning bolt, Tlaloc's power waned, and as he doubted himself, his power fell. Inevitable defeat, and foolishness to think otherwise. Storms, however, are unpredictable, and knowing her brother the way she did, Chalchiuhtlicue took a single action that would help her brother win. She called for her brother's attention, leaned over, and kissed Tezcatlipoca.

Saying Tlaloc felt fury would be quite the understatement. He felt embarrassment, anger, regret. All the emotions and mistakes he had been holding onto bled from him. He remembered how he overreacted, he remembered how Mictlantecuhtli let his embarrassment manifest, and he remembered all the rage of knowing that his sister was in love with an awful person. He conjured all his pain and frustrations and emotions into a single bolt of lightning, and struck at Mictlantecuhtli.

The lightning bolt nearly turned him to dust. The force was so great, even Tlaloc was thrown to the ground, and from then on, when anyone had anything negative to say to Tlaloc, they kept it to themselves.

Cuāuhtli-ītl

Pronounced: [Kwow-tlee-EETL]

Meaning: Eagle-Wind or Storm-Lightning

Used by: Tlaloc

Appearance: A blinding flash tearing across the sky, followed by the roar of thunder; often described in Nahua poetry as the jagged claw of an eagle or the breath of the gods.

Fun Fact: In Classical Nahuatl, the most common words for lightning are *ītlāloc* (meaning "fire of Tlaloc") and *huitztli*, meaning "spark" or "lightning bolt." Many of these terms connect lightning directly to divine activity, particularly to Tlaloc, the God of Rain.

History: To the Nahua peoples, lightning was never just a flash of light; it was a divine message, a weapon of the gods, a crack in the world between realms. In myth, lightning bolts were hurled by gods like Tlaloc or his warrior attendants, the Tlaloque, to fertilize the Earth with sacred rain. Some sources suggest that where lightning struck the ground was where maize could grow strongest, and lightning-struck places were seen as spiritually powerful. Lightning was also viewed as an omen: the arrival of storms marked the favor or fury of the gods, and in some versions of Aztec cosmology, it was said that the gods of storms and lightning carried souls to the afterlife when struck.

CHAPTER 19
CLAWS VS. SIN

Next to enter the battlefield was Itzpapalotl, the Obsidian Butterfly, and Tlazolteotl, the Filth Goddess.

This was no battle of strangers. This was a battle of sisters. Of Tonantzin. Of warriors who had once fought side by side, and now stood face to face under the pale-moon-sky of the Divine Flower War.

Tlazolteotl was feared across the lands not because of her strength, but because of what she knew. There were no such things as secrets around her, and this made her a threat to all.

She created sin, and she purified it. She could consume sin, and transform it. She fought with a strange, beautiful fury, dancing with blades made of sharpened bone and teeth. No one could read the sins of an enemy better than she. And once she saw the shame in your heart, she would use it to destroy you.

Itzpapalotl was different. She did not play mind games, nor did she care what you had done in the shadows.

She was there to meet you in combat, wherever you chose to fight. Still, she would be lying if she said she didn't feel some tinge of fear during this battle. She viewed herself as strong, and for others to know her secrets, and her regrets? That was truly a great fear. And fear wasn't something she often felt. Before the battle, they bowed, but said nothing. No parting words, or threats or jeers.

The two were quiet, which confused many. These two goddesses were a lot of things, but quiet was never used to describe either.

The battle began with an explosion of sound: Itzpapalotl dashed forward, claws bared, but as she reached Itzpapalotl, the memories inside flooded back in. Her claws dashing off the head of the Deer Woman. The gurgles and the screams. The pain of regret flooded back, and Itzpapalotl crashed into the floor. She could not harm Tlazolteotl.

She was sure this would cost her the battle, but when Tlazolteotl stepped forward, she did not strike with a dagger, but with a hug. Tlazolteotl embraced her sister, holding her trembling body, and offering her forgiveness. Yes, Tlazolteotl was the basin of sin from which all drank, but she was just as well the great forgiver.

All the pain and madness she had poured out of her, not as sweat, but as black ooze. Steam lifted from her body, and though it was difficult, and though she cried, in time, she felt better.

The struggle of this battle was not easy for either of them, and when it was over, Itzpapalotl rose, stronger than she had ever been before. Tlazolteotl, however, was exhausted, and fell to the floor in a heavy slumber.

Temazcal

Pronounced: [Teh-MAZ-kal]

Meaning: House of Heat (from Nahuatl *temaz* "steam" and *calli* "house")

Type of: Sacred steam bath, healing ritual, spiritual rebirth chamber

Appearance: A small, dome-shaped stone structure, often made of adobe or volcanic rock, with a single low entrance and a central pit for hot stones. Steam was created by pouring water infused with herbs over the stones.

Fun Fact: Warriors, midwives, and priests all used the *temazcal* for purification. It was considered a physical, mental, and spiritual reset.

History: The *temazcal* was an essential part of Aztec life, tied to medicine, ritual, and mythology. It was more than just a sweat bath, it was a ceremonial space of rebirth and cleansing. Women gave birth near or inside *temazcales*, believing the heat would ease labor and that the structure mimicked the womb. Warriors used it to purify themselves after battle, cleansing blood, sin, and fear. Herbal steam prepared by healers was used to treat wounds, fevers, or spiritual afflictions. Shamans conducted guided rituals inside, where participants would sweat out impurities and confront visions or inner truths. Today, *temazcales* are still used in many Indigenous communities across Mexico and Central America as a symbol of healing, connection, and an ancestral tradition.

CHAPTER 20
MAGIC VS. BONES

Tezcatlipoca, the Smoking Mirror, was the God of Sorcery, of Shadows, of War, and Trickery. He had no throne and wanted no master. He was the ambition of the gods, the mind behind every scheme, every betrayal, every victory earned not by strength but by cleverness.

But if Tezcatlipoca was ambition made flesh, Mictecacihuatl was death made permanent. She was the Queen of the Dead, ruler of Mictlan, and wielder of absolute silence. Hers was the domain none escaped from. She saw all things end, and in those endings, she found peace. Her calm unnerved even the wildest gods, and her gaze could cause instant death to the weak-hearted.

Mictecacihuatl stood motionless. Her skin pale as ash, her robes made of bone. A necklace of eyes hung around her neck, not for vanity, but so she could see the truth from every angle. Her voice was rarely used, but when she spoke, the sound echoed like it was coming from the bottom of a cave.

Tezcatlipoca arrived with smoke in his footsteps. A jaguar walked at his side, then turned to ash. His body shimmered, never fully here or there, his face hidden behind the obsidian mirror that gave him his name. He smiled, but it was not a smile of joy. It was the grin of a player holding a card no one else could see.

The Goddess of the Dead bowed her head once, and only slightly. The God of Magic did the same. This was the only courtesy they would offer each other.

Mictecacihuatl struck first, raising a strange smiling dagger in her hand. This dagger bore eyes and a face, and eternal hunger for the living. The dagger opened its mouth, and all that was living was killed. No wind. No sound. No animals. No plants. Everything, both living or otherwise, had ceased. The only living thing that still stood was Tezcatlipoca.

Tezcatlipoca raised his mirror, and ten copies of himself appeared, each real, each laughing. They circled her, throwing daggers and bolts of magic, yet she did not flinch. Her necklace of eyes saw everything, and so she moved, with little effort, to avoid his attacks.

Tezcatlipoca attacked with everything he had, and it was not enough. Mictecacihuatl could see all, and everything he did meant nothing. Exhaustion set in, and when it did, the Lady of the Dead made her attack. She raised her dagger again, and the life of Tezcatlipoca was pulled out of him.

Mictecacihuatl had won.

Tezcacuitlapilli

Pronounced: [Tess-ka-kweet-la-PEEL-lee]

Meaning: Obsidian-Spined Tail or Mirror-Tail Blade (interpretations vary)

Type of: Sacrificial dagger, ritual weapon

Appearance: A short, curved blade made of flint or obsidian, its hilt often carved into the shape of a human or divine face, complete with wide eyes and an open mouth as if in a scream or chant. Some versions have decorative feathers, turquoise inlays, and symbolic etchings across the blade.

Fun Fact: Many surviving sacrificial daggers feature anthropomorphic designs not just for beauty, but to give the blade a spiritual presence, as if the knife itself bore witness to the offering.

History: The tezcacuitlapilli was used in religious rituals, especially human sacrifices performed to nourish the gods. Its short, strong shape was ideal for swift and precise cuts across the chest. The carved face on the hilt was more than decoration, it represented the blade as a living extension of the god. In some rituals, the dagger was treated as an honored participant, cleansed, adorned, and even spoken to as if it had a soul. Eyes and mouths carved into the handle were believed to let the blade "see" the offering and "speak" to the gods.

CHAPTER 21

THE DEAL

Tezcatlipoca awoke from his vision with an angered gasp, stepping away from the Staff of Sight, and at once began a solution to his problem. Over and over again, every solution he saw ended with Mictecacihuatl defeating him. He could not defeat her, no matter how hard he tried. Her power was too great, and her necklace was too strong. There was no way he could defeat her, at least not now. In time he could craft a weapon, he supposed, but to do so now would drain too much of his magic. He would beat her, but would then certainly lose all battles after.

The only way to win this battle was to avoid the battle altogether. To do this, however, required the greatest scheme he had ever schemed. It required a promise that none could know, but it was a promise he knew Mictecacihuatl could not say no to.

Behind closed doors, where others could not hear, Tezcatlipoca approached Mictecacihuatl and Mictlantecuhtli and offered them a deal he knew they would not refuse. Should he become king, he would conjure his greatest creation yet: a race of massive beings who would populate the land. He would plant an evil, deep in their hearts, that would fester eternal and this evil was called: greed.

They would lust for all the things they could and could not have. Money, food, men, women. They would lust for land, and when they had all they wanted, they would still be unsatisfied. An endless hunger, never to be sated.

He would plant this greed into their very beings, but when they died, this greed would die with them. When their souls entered the great beyond of Mictlan, they would enter as better people. These beings would be a problem for the living, but a blessing for the dead.

Great giant skeletons to worship the King and Queen of the Dead, en masse, for all eternity. The deal was too good to refuse. Yet, one final stipulation had to be made. Once a year, for every year from now until eternity, the dead would be allowed to return to the land of the living.

When the time came for the battle to take place, Tezcatlipoca arrived, and Mictecacihuatl did not. And so the God of Magic won his first battle without ever having to fight.

Día de Muertos

Pronounced: [DEE-ah deh MWEHR-tohs]

Meaning: Day of the Dead

Type of: Ancestral celebration, remembrance ritual, cultural festival

Appearance: A vibrant display of marigold petals (*cempasúchil*), flickering candles, sugar skulls, *papel picado* banners, food offerings, and personal altars (*ofrendas*) adorned with photographs and gifts for the dead.

Fun Fact: Día de Muertos is not a somber funeral, it is a joyous reunion. Families believe the spirits of loved ones return each year to visit, eat, drink, and laugh with the living.

History: Día de Muertos is one of the most iconic and enduring celebrations in Mesoamerican culture. Its roots trace back thousands of years to the Aztec, Maya, Purépecha, and other Indigenous civilizations who honored the dead not with fear, but with reverence. The Aztec held rituals to honor Mictecacihuatl, Lady of the Dead, and Mictlantecuhtli, Lord of the Dead, believing the dead continued their journey through the afterlife.

When Catholicism arrived, these ancestral rites merged with All Saints' Day and All Souls' Day to form the hybrid tradition we know today. Celebrated on November 1 and 2, the first day honors children and infants (*Día de los Inocentes*), while the second honors adults. Altars are built in homes and cemeteries, decorated with food, drink, favorite belongings, and spiritual symbols to guide the dead home.

CHAPTER 22
SHIELD VS. CLAWS

They called one the Shield Hand. The other, the Obsidian Butterfly. Two of the most dangerous goddesses in all creation. One stood tall and unshaken, her body hardened like stone, unbreakable, unstoppable, unbending. The other was sleek and ferocious, cloaked in night and razor wings, forged for the sole purpose of destruction. There would be no tricks. No clever misdirection. This was going to be a test of weapon against wall, fang against armor, obsidian against divine flesh.

Itzpapalotl descended like a shadow you thought you saw in the corner of your eye. Her wings scraped the air, blades of pure obsidian sharpened against the bones of monsters and foes alike. Chimalma stood waiting, shield on her arm, unflinching. She braced herself for the incoming attack, and though fear was in her mind, bravery was there as well.

Itzpapalotl struck first, a blur of wings and claws. She danced around Chimalma, carving through air, testing the shield, looking for weakness. At first, there was none. Every slash bounced off her skin or was deflected with a twist of her wrist. It seemed, for a moment, that nothing would ever touch her.

But Itzpapalotl wasn't just a warrior. She was an artist of death. She noticed the smallest details: the way Chimalma's shoulder flinched when the blades grazed too close, the way she shifted her footing slightly when hit with something sharp. Obsidian. That was the answer. Obsidian didn't just scratch, it sank. Not deep. Not enough to kill. But enough to hurt. Enough to make her bleed.

Chimalma felt it too. She didn't panic, but she adjusted. Her breathing changed. Her movements slowed. For the first time in centuries, she was taking damage. Small cuts. Thin slivers. But death, even in pieces, can find a way in. Itzpapalotl pressed the advantage, slicing low, then high, wings flaring like meteors. One cut slashed across Chimalma's side. Another across her shield arm.

It looked like Itzpapalotl would win.

But Chimalma was not forged to be pretty, she was forged to protect, to endure. She gritted her teeth and took the blows, marching forward through the storm of strikes. Each step left a trail of blood, but she kept going. Her arm, once raised to block, now moved to grab. She waited for one mistake, just one. It was all she needed. She just needed her to make one mistake and—

Itzpapalotl came in too fast, too confident, and for a single second, she misjudged her distance. That was all Chimalma needed. Her hand shot out and grabbed Itzpapalotl by the wrist. Pulling her in close, she threw her over her shoulder onto the ground. Her foot planted to hold her in place, Chimalma crushed Itzpapalotl's chest in one single devastating strike.

Chimalma stood over her, bloodied but breathing. She turned and walked away, hand on her side, blood still dripping from the hundreds of cuts on her body. She had won. Not because she was faster, not because she was stronger, but because she could take the pain and keep going.

The Obsidian Butterfly had cut her, but the Shield had held.

Itzli

Pronounced: [EETS-lee]

Meaning: Obsidian or Blade

Type of: Sacred material and symbolic element

Appearance: Jet-black volcanic glass, sharp and reflective, often carved into blades, mirrors, or ceremonial tools.

Fun Fact: Obsidian can be sharpened to a molecular edge, far sharper than steel. Even today, some surgeons use obsidian scalpels for extremely fine cuts.

History: In Nahua cosmology, Itzli (obsidian) was not just a tool, but a material of power and spiritual resonance. It was used to craft knives for ritual sacrifice, scrying mirrors for prophecy, and arrowheads for divine warfare. Itzli carried the power to cut both flesh and magic. Obsidian was believed to hold memory and spirit, its reflective surface a gateway between worlds.

CHAPTER 23
GRUDGE MATCH

Tlaloc and Tezcatlipoca had not spoken in a very long time. Their silence echoed louder than thunder, louder than war. When the match was announced, all rushed to watch it. Their tension had lingered in the air like smoke, and now it would finally ignite. This wasn't just a battle of strength or magic, this was a grudge match between two rivals.

Tlaloc stepped into the arena with great ceremony: he descended from a cloud, adorned with fine garments, a spear of trickling lightning, and attended by his many Tlaloque. Lightning wrapped around his body, his breath misted with storm, and he wore a grin of victory. There was nothing Tezcatlipoca could do to win this battle, at least not in his mind.

Tezcatlipoca had won his previous battle through trickery, and Tlaloc was convinced he would try such a thing again. But trickery would only lead to anger, and anger was what fueled Tlaloc. Even now, his powers rippled around his body as a side effect of his growing rage toward the God of Darkness.

He had prepared himself for anything Tezcatlipoca and his magic could or would do, and he was ready to destroy it without mercy. Nothing would stop Tlaloc from his rise, and he was ready to show the world that.

Across from him, Tezcatlipoca stood calm, adorned in simple regalia, and carried a single mask in his hand. Tezcatlipoca knew that Tlaloc was ready for battle, but his preparation was with Tezcatlipoca, with Magic. Tlaloc had no preparations whatsoever for anything other than what Tezcatlipoca was. And so, that is exactly who Tlaloc would fight—someone who wasn't Tezcatlipoca.

The God of Magic crafted a mask that would transform not just his body, but his mind. A person nearly entirely different from who he was, who had no magic, but great speed and strength. Tezcatlipoca now became the God of Rivals, Yaotl, whose very strength came from rivalries and battles.

Before Tlaloc could even raise a voice to complain about what had unfolded, Yaotl had made his move. He dashed forward at speeds that rivaled Itzpapalotl's. Tlaloc threw his magic and his lightning and his rain, but none of that mattered.

The fog to blind Tezcatlipoca was a minor obstacle for the charging Yaotl.

The rain to cause confusion did nothing but cool the hot sweat off the brow of Yaotl.

The lightning meant to strike down Tezcatlipoca was evaded by the quick steps of Yaotl.

Nothing Tlaloc did mattered, and the rage he had felt misplaced against this stranger.

All the banter and rude remarks Tlaloc had prepared for meant nothing against Yaotl. He expected to gloat and play mind games with Tezcatlipoca. He had intended to mock him and belittle him, building up his own rage and anger.

But to Yaotl? They were empty words.

With a weapon in hand, Yaotl buried his blade in the chest of Tlaloc. The God of Storms had fallen to a foe whose name he didn't even know.

Yaotl

Pronounced: [YAH-ohtl]

Meaning: Enemy or Warrior

Type of: Aspect of Tezcatlipoca

Appearance: A tall, shadow-draped figure with obsidian war paint across his chest, carrying a *macuahuitl* and wearing the eagle-feathered headdress of an elite warrior.

Fun Fact: Yaotl is not a separate god, but a battlefield incarnation of Tezcatlipoca, used to represent his presence in war, strife, and personal combat. In fact, Tezcatlipoca has over a hundred names and aspects in Aztec mythology.

History: Yaotl appears throughout Nahua texts as a title meaning "enemy" or "combatant," but in myth, it specifically refers to one of Tezcatlipoca's most fearsome warlike forms. In this shape, Tezcatlipoca walked the Earth as a challenger, entering conflicts to test the strength, resolve, and heart of gods and men alike. Many Aztec warriors were given the title *yaotl* in reference to this aspect, marking them as chosen by the god. In stories and poetry, Yaotl is often invoked as a dark spirit of strength, and it is said that when you felt a sudden chill in the middle of a battle, the enemy was watching.

CHAPTER 24

THE FINAL BATTLE

The final battle was here. The ultimate showdown was ready to begin. The winner of this contest would be crowned the God King. Would it be the Goddess of Shields, brave and strong? Or would the God of Magic, and his trickery, prove useful one more time?

Tezcatlipoca.
Chimalma.
The God of Magic.
The Goddess of Shields.
Brain.
Brawn.
Let the battle begin.

Chimalma did not wait for Tezcatlipoca to strike, and for the first time in the tournament, she rushed forward. She wielded her shield like a weapon, bound tightly to her arm, and carried it with insurmountable raw strength. Like a mountain stampeding forward, Chimalma raged forward, shouting her warrior call, and crashed hard into Tezcatlipoca.

At once, Tezcatlipoca threw on his Yaotl mask, and the two warriors clashed. Strength versus Strength, warrior versus warrior. Yaotl was diabolical in his relentless strikes, but Chimalma held her ground. Yaotl may have been the God of Rivals, and a warrior of great strength, but he lacked one thing of vital importance: wisdom. Yaotl was, for all purposes, a warrior with very little experience. He had fought Tlaloc, but that was it. He had never met another warrior on the field, and certainly never one of the caliber of Chimalma.

Chimalma faced Yaotl warrior to warrior, and when Yaotl overstepped, she crushed her shield into his face and sent him sprawling backward.

Yaotl returned to his previous form, appearing as Tezcatlipoca once again. In this form, he summoned jaguars and illusions, which carved and struck at Chimalma, but nothing worse than she had already faced with Itzpapalotl. For all of his power, Tezcatlipoca had become his own worst enemy.

While it was true that he could see the future, and any variations of this future, his ability to change and create infinite solutions meant he had to prepare for infinite outcomes. The more ideas he had, the more outcomes there were, and this meant more preparation.

He had tried to see the future, but due to his own power, the future was simply too vast for him to see. It was then that he had to rely on his raw talent, which, to be clear, he had in abundance. Yes, he was a trickster and a schemer, but do not confuse a strategist with someone who cannot take immediate action. A preference for hesitation did not mean he was incapable of instant action.

Chapter 24: The Final Battle

Tezcatlipoca conjured spells, and summoned weapons, and all of them were effective, but never quite effective enough. He was at war with a wall, and while you can hit a wall with a great many things, a wall is still a wall. A wall doesn't need grace, it doesn't need plans.

Chimalma was battered, and bruised, but for every attack against her, she struck Tezcatlipoca back. If he sliced her with a blade, she clobbered him with her shield. Over and over, time after time, the two traded attacks. Chimalma's stamina vs. Tezcatlipoca's ambition. One would break, the other would hold.

It was Chimalma who would break first, but destiny can be fickle, and some things that should be kept hidden are found by accident. While yes, Chimalma did fall first, it was Tezcatlipoca who hesitated to strike. Standing above Chimalma, a vision came to him.

It was a vision of himself, kneeling down in defeat, looking up at another god. A god of green and white, of heroes and justice. A god who would defeat Tezcatlipoca, and end his reign as God King. A god of kindness, not fear, and a god whose being entirely existed because of Chimalma.

Tezcatlipoca was standing over the mother of his future enemy, and in this moment Tezcatlipoca saw the beginning of his end. He saw his reign, he saw his victory, and he saw its end.

Seeing this distraction, though having no idea about the vision itself, Chimalma slammed her shield into Tezcatlipoca's leg. The same leg that hid the magical obsidian which held back the curse of Chaos. When her shield hit the obsidian, the obsidian broke, and from that gaping wound, Chaos was unleashed.

The creeping, crawling, cursed Chaos had returned, and it consumed the body of Tezcatlipoca.

Chimalxochitl

Pronounced: [Chee-mahl-SHO-cheetl]

Meaning: Shield Flower; more accurately, this refers to a sunflower

Type of: Royalty, the first Aztec Princess

Appearance: Like all princesses, she would have worn a *Huipilli*, which is a type of richly embroidered blouse, and a *Cueitl*, which is a type of skirt. While we don't have details of specific articles of jewelry, she likely wore gold, turquoise, and *huitzil* feathers in her hair and on her body.

Fun Fact: Chimalxochitl is known as one of the earliest recorded noblewomen in central Mexico, often described in post-classic Nahua annals as the "first Aztec princess." She was the daughter of a Toltec ruler and is remembered for her role in uniting Toltec and Chichimec bloodlines during a formative time in central highland politics. Her name appears in several sources as a symbol of the cultural and political fusion between ancient civilizations and the emerging Nahua dynasties.

Chapter 24: The Final Battle

History: Nobody knows the fate of Chimalxochitl, as her story is shrouded in a lot of folklore. During a war, the Aztec royal family was captured, but what happened after that is unknown. Some say that Chimalxochitl died in a fire of her own making, refusing to die as a prisoner. Others say she was forced into marriage with a prince, and eventually led their people as a powerful and respected queen.

CHAPTER 25

AND THE WINNER IS...

The creeping, crawling, cursed Chaos had returned, and it consumed the body of Tezcatlipoca.

It poured from the crack of his wounded leg like venom from a broken fang, a writhing storm of screaming darkness that twisted the god into something unrecognizable. His limbs swelled and blackened, his eyes burned white-hot, and the jaguar within him howled with bloodlust and hunger.

The battlefield trembled beneath the weight of his transformation. Gods watching from above pulled back, uncertain if they were witnessing a coronation or a catastrophe. Some even sought to interfere, but the rules were quite clear. This was Chimalma's battle to win or lose.

Tezcatlipoca's body became a war zone of shifting shapes: claws and fangs, smoke and flame, obsidian shards and ancient curses. There was no strategy now. No calculation.

Only instinct, raw and wild. He was truly an all-consuming God of Chaos.

But Chimalma did not run.

Though battered, bruised, and nearly broken, she stood. She saw the Chaos spewing from the wound, not as a curse, but as a wound crying out to be sealed. She understood what needed to be done, she just needed the strength to do it.

The two battled, with the Chaos and its endless mouths and endless claws attacking Chimalma, and Chimalma doing her best not to die. She struck back at the Chaos, fighting with all her strength, and when she saw her opportunity, she took it.

Without hesitation, Chimalma tore the shield from her arm, tearing her arm off with it, and drove it directly into the wound in Tezcatlipoca's leg. The divine object forged in ages past sealed the Chaos like a lid upon a jar, choking the darkness back into silence.

The battlefield fell still, the Chaos was halted, and Chimalma lay defeated on the ground.

Tezcatlipoca, gasping, staggered back into his human form, his breathing ragged, his skin scorched.

Tezcatlipoca had won, but at what cost? The other gods did not respect him, they feared him. He did not win of his own will, but the will of the Chaos. His greatest secret was now bared to all.

Chapter 25: And the Winner Is...

There were no cheers, no drums, and no songs to mark the rise of a king.

The gods stood silent as Tezcatlipoca took his throne, and as he sat, the others bowed their heads. They bowed, but not out of joy, nor even respect. They bowed out of fear. They had seen what slept beneath his skin: they had seen the Chaos. And though it was sealed once more, they knew it could return.

Tezcatlipoca had claimed victory.

But there was no glory in it.

He was now king.

But there were no willing subjects.

The gods left. One by one. Not a word spoken.

And Tezcatlipoca remained.

Alone.

The new King of the Gods.

Crowned by Chaos.

The Era of the First Sun had begun.

Mexica

Pronounced: [Meh-SHEE-kah]

Meaning: The People of Mexico; the name from which "Mexico" is derived

Fun Fact: The Mexica never referred to themselves as "Azteca." That name was invented by later historians and popularized in European texts. "Mexica" was their proper name, and they saw themselves as chosen wanderers, guided by prophecy to build the greatest empire in Mesoamerica.

History: The Mexica were a Nahua-speaking people who arrived in the Valley of Mexico in the thirteenth century after migrating from a northern land they called Aztlan. Considered uncivilized by the city-states they encountered, they were at first marginalized, settling on the swampy islands of Lake Texcoco. There, they claimed to receive a vision from their patron god Huitzilopochtli, who commanded them to build a city where they saw an eagle on a cactus devouring a snake. That city was Tenochtitlan, the heart of the Mexica Empire.

PART 4

A HISTORY LESSON

The myths of the gods are only one part of the story. To understand them fully, we must also understand the people who carried their names forward, those we now call the Aztec. But that name itself is a modern invention. The people we call Aztec called themselves Mexica, and their history has often been told not by them, but by the conquerors who destroyed their world.

Part 4 explores the truth behind the names, the legacy of the Mexica, and the violent rewriting of their story by the Spanish. This section is not myth, but historical reflection, an attempt to separate fact from fiction, and to honor the culture, beauty, and resilience of a civilization whose voice still echoes in its descendants today.

CHAPTER 26

THE AZTEC DIDN'T CALL THEMSELVES THE AZTEC

There was no Aztec Empire. There was no Aztec mythology. There was never a time in Mesoamerican history where anyone ever referred to themselves as Aztec. The mythology you'll find in this book actually comes from the Mexica people (Meh-she-kah). So if they weren't called the Aztec, why do we call them that? Why would an Indigenous nation call themselves one thing, but the world as a whole refers to them as something else?

If you love history, you already know the reason why. It's always the same reason why.

"Colonizer bullshit?"

Yep.

Colonizer bullshit.

In the 1800s, three centuries after the Aztec Empire had fallen, a European scholar named Alexander von Humboldt used the term Azteca to describe these people, referencing their ancestral ties to Aztlan. Now, to his credit, the Aztec (Mexica) did have a holy land they referred to as Aztlan. The Aztec believed that they had originally come from this land and one day they would go back. Therefore, they were the people from Aztlan: the Azteca (or Aztec). It makes sense, I get it, but here's the thing: the Aztec *never* called themselves that.

They were the Mexica Empire, part of the larger Nahua people, which in itself is part of the larger land of Mesoamerica. To call them the Aztec is not technically wrong, but it's certainly not right either. It's complicated, and nuanced, for several reasons.

For example, my brother and my dad are both named Daniel. You'd think that makes my brother "Junior," but legally, my parents never added Junior, so he's just Steven (his middle name). Calling him Junior isn't right—but it's not technically wrong. He is, technically, a junior, as he does have our father's name. And throughout his life, he has been called Junior by several people, which he admittedly isn't a fan of.

I'm going to call them the Aztec and I already know what you're going to say.

Chapter 26: The Aztec Didn't Call Themselves the Aztec

"Aren't you perpetuating the misinformed name by continuing to call them the Aztec?"

Look, I get that argument, but here's the thing: You probably had no idea that the Aztec were called the Mexica when you picked up this book. If you had seen a book about something you never heard of, you probably would be less likely to grab it. *Myths, Gods, and Rituals of Mexica Mythology*? It's just less likely to sell, and as educationally authentic as that may be to call it that, if nobody reads your book, then who is ever going to know? Aztec, though? You know the name, you already have some idea of the stuff you'll find inside this book. And now that you're here, I can break down that misconception.

So yeah, it's not technically right to call them the Aztec, but that's what we call them now, that's what the world knows them as, and that's just the way it is.

It's not fair, it's not right, but it's with baby steps that we can move forward with a little more knowledge than we did before, and who knows? If we spread that knowledge far and wide, maybe one day we can finally put to bed the Aztec name and call them by their real name: the Mexica.

Mexica (Meh-shee-kah) sure looks a lot like the word Mexico, and that's no coincidence. The country of Mexico is named after the Aztec Empire under its original name, meaning it's not pronounced Mex-e-co or Meh-he-co, it's Meh-she-co. The inspiration doesn't end there, either—the Mexican flag includes one too. The eagle holding a snake standing on a prickly pear cactus? That comes from an Aztec legend, the founding of Tenochtitlan (Teh-knowch-teet-lawn). It was believed that the Aztec people built their kingdom on the exact spot they saw that image: an eagle with a snake clutched in its claws while perched on a prickly pear cactus. In fact, their capital city's name, Tenochtitlan, meant the Land of the Prickly Pear Cactus.

That flag isn't the only one to do this, either. The Aztlan flag, or the Chicano Movement flag, otherwise known as the United Farm Workers Union flag, features a minimalist version of the perched eagle. It is a reminder of the Indigenous history of the Mexican people, especially Mexican Americans. To this day, people across the country, though most often in California, fly this flag as a way to tell everyone they aren't just Mexican, they are Mexican-American, and they are proud of their Indigenous heritage.

The "Aztec Empire" wasn't ruled by a single kingdom, but consisted of three cities: Tenochtitlan (Teh-knowch-teet-lawn), Texcoco (Tesh-coco), and Tlacopan (Tlah-co-pon). Together, they formed what historians now call the Triple Alliance—a military and economic coalition that conquered, taxed, and ruled over much of central Mexico. The three cities ruled over several smaller kingdoms, making the Aztec Empire not a single kingdom, but hundreds of various kingdoms, all with their own dialects and languages, their own mythologies, and their own cultures. Many of these Indigenous cultures, including the Mexica, exist to this day.

CHAPTER 27
"SAVAGES LIVING IN TREES"

The Aztec were not heroes, and they were not villains. They weren't good, they weren't bad. They were, like many empires throughout history, complicated. Yet, when most people look at the Aztec, they have this preconceived notion of them as jungle-dwelling barbarians who ran around naked and sacrificed people by the thousands.

Let's start with the whole "Aztec living in trees and swamps" myth, because this is probably the most egregiously incorrect myth and the easiest to disprove. The Aztec capital was Tenochtitlan, and it was the third largest city in the entire world at the time, in terms of both population and scale. Tenochtitlan translates to "the Place of the Prickly Pear Cactus." *Tenoch* = prickly pear cactus, *Titlan* = place of. Tenochtitlan had a population of nearly 250,000, and was a man-made floating city. Never before, or ever again, has there been a floating city to the scale of Tenochtitlan.

There were gardens, one of the world's first zoos, aqueducts that brought in fresh water from the mountains, a marketplace with hundreds of stores, a pyramid castle, and so much more. Hernan Cortes himself, the mastermind behind the Spanish invasion, was quoted as saying that Tenochtitlan was one of the most beautiful sights he had ever seen.

"What happened to Tenochtitlan?" you might be asking. The Spaniards built a city on top of it: Mexico City. Because that's what invaders do. They state how beautiful something is, acknowledge how it is a world wonder—then build something on top of it so you forget it ever existed.

Imagine constructing one of the most beautiful cities in world history—the biggest man-made floating city ever built—and a few centuries later, everyone not only forgets about it, they think you lived in trees.

As for running around half-naked, there's some truth to that one, but not in the way you probably think. Take the idea of *Apocalypto* out of your mind—though, frankly, people should have known better than to expect historical accuracy and care from the director—but I digress. For commoners, men wore various combinations of loincloths, skirts, cloaks, and shirts. Women wore dresses or skirts with shirts.

Many people wore sandals, but not everyone. Often, clothes were white or beige with few accessories, as specific clothing colors were reserved for specific careers. Hair styles were also important, with specific hairstyles conveying status, such as whether you were a priest, a warrior, a farmer, or whether you were married. Short hair was uncommon for both men and women.

In many instances, especially for farmers, it was common for both men and women alike to not wear shirts, revealing their chests, and to wear only a loincloth. To the Aztec, a woman showing her breasts wasn't seen as immoral or even sexual. This changed when the Spaniards arrived and the Catholic Church implemented modesty laws.

For those who weren't commoners, colorful clothes, feathers, body paint, and jewelry were used to convey their social status or career. Priests and royals had earrings, nose rings, lip rings, and body paint. Body paint was very common and often correlated to either a festival or their career. Once again, hair style was important, and there were certain hair styles only royals could wear.

In times of war, the commoner soldier would not change his clothing by much. If he had the means, he wore a padded shirt or cloak, but that was it. Elite warriors wore full armor: a helmet, a shield, and padded body armor. One of the reasons the Aztec wore very little armor was because the bladed weapons they used were made with obsidian. Obsidian is 300 times sharper than steel. To the Aztec, it was better to learn how to dodge than to rely on armor. As such, their fighting styles changed to accommodate the weaponry, and as such, armor wasn't as important.

This is all to say: yes, they did "run around half-naked," but the half that wasn't naked was often covered with beautiful feathers, gold and jade jewelry, or elaborate body paint designs.

CHAPTER 28
BLOOD ON THEIR HANDS

Now we get to the part where we, without any beating around the bush, address the horrible things they did. It's not my job to romanticize the Aztec; it's my job to present to you their empire and culture the way it was. Sometimes, it's not pretty. That's history.

Yes, the Aztec did sacrifice people. They were a warrior nation before they became an empire.

Everything they had, and everything they built, they built on the fact that they were the best warriors on their side of the world. Even when they had conquered most of the land and there were few left to wage war with, they created Flower Wars. Think of it like early combat sports: Two trained military units met on a battlefield, with the intent not to kill, but to capture. Capturing an enemy unit meant fame for you and political power for your kingdom. They held these tournaments every so often, not only to excite viewers and those who gambled, but also to remind everyone that they had the best warriors.

Even though these Flower Wars did not result in immediate death, unless their kingdom bought their freedom, the captured soldiers were sacrificed.

These captured soldiers were first taken to an arena, tied to a heavy stone, and given a blunt weapon to defend themselves. If they survived the onslaught of armed soldiers, they earned their freedom. Almost nobody earned their freedom; it was a carrot on a stick. After which, the warriors would be taken to the local temple and have their hearts literally ripped out. Brutal, violent, and bloody.

Other sacrifices included the following. Before you read, however, I give you a fair warning. Some of these are violent and cruel, even by the standards of the time. Read at your discretion. These are not for the faint of heart:

- **Ritual of Tezcatlipoca:** An individual is chosen, always a man. For one year, he is given a life of grandeur. He is given riches, power, women, men, and anything else he'd like. He, in essence, lives like a king. He holds no actual power or sway, but he is treated very well. After that year is up, he is taken to the temple and has his heart ripped out while he is still alive.

- **Ritual of Xipe Totec:** Often prisoners of war, individuals would be taken to the temple and flayed alive. This means they had their skin removed from their body, often as one large piece. This would be done by priests who would be wearing actual human skin suits. The priests would then wear these new skin suits for a whole month.

- **Ritual of Tlaloc:** This involved drowning a child. This was not a punishment, nor were children taken against their will. This was, as most rituals are, a privilege for the sacrificed individual. Nobles and royals often sacrificed their own children, as dying in this way sent them straight to the Thirteen Heavens, bypassing Mictlan, the underworld.

Many sacrifices, however, did not involve murder. Many involved sacrificing flowers, fish, and corn. In fact, many Aztec gods did not like sacrificing humans. As we will discuss later, there were battles fought between the gods over whether to sacrifice humans.

You'll notice that, on that list, there was no "mass-sacrificing thousands of people in a single day." Because that never happened. Famously, a Spanish friar named Diego Duran made the claim that 80,400 people were sacrificed over the course of four days. That is fourteen people sacrificed every minute, for four days straight. Obviously, this wasn't true. That's not to say sacrifices en masse didn't occur; they did, especially during wartime. But 80,000 people? Insane.

At the height of the Aztec Empire, when they were in the middle of wartime, they could sacrifice, at most, 1,000 people over the course of a week or two. It's a lot of people, no doubt, but not 80,000.

While 1,000 people sacrificed in a time of war is a high number, it's certainly not record-setting, especially for Europeans. Thus, calling them savages based on this simply isn't fair.

The Romans sacrificed people in the Colosseum for entertainment, yet many people glorify that, rather than condemn it. When the Aztec do it, and for religious reasons, they are often seen as barbarians. This isn't to say that what the Aztec did wasn't, through a modern moral lens, "bad," but that, if we're going to view what the Aztec did through a modern moral lens, we should do the same for others. Case in point: the Reign of Terror.

In 1793, in just a single year, the French revolutionary government executed nearly 40,000 people. This was not a war. They were not soldiers. These were innocent civilians being executed by terrorists. While a lot of those people died in varying ways, we do have a few specific death tolls to point out. 16,000 people were publicly executed via guillotine, with crowds of thousands gathering to watch. When a head was chopped off, people tossed it around in the crowd. 10,000 people died in jail due to harsh conditions. 6,000 people were killed via drowning. This all happened in a single year. It was a horrible, awful thing that the French did, yet many still say it was a necessary evil. It did create the foundations for democracy, after all. But are the French seen today as savages? Certainly not.

CHAPTER 29

THE MASSACRES

It is estimated that over the course of three years, between 1519 and 1521, the Spanish forces massacred over 20,000 innocent people: non-soldiers, women, children, and the elderly.

- **The Massacre of Toxcatl:** When a festival for their gods was to be held, between 1,000 and 5,000 people showed up to celebrate—and were killed. Pedro de Alvarado was responsible for this, and he himself attended the event as a guest. Why did he do it? Nobody knows. Many believe he did it to steal the gold jewelry off their bodies. Pedro himself says he was trying to "stop a sacrifice." Stop a sacrifice...by killing thousands of unarmed people.

- **The Massacre of Cholula:** 6,000 or more innocent civilians were killed by Hernan Cortes. After they had invited him to their city, Hernan grew suspicious that an assassination plot was brewing. No attempt was made, but that didn't stop Hernan from "preemptive revenge."

- **Massacre at Tepeaca:** Death toll unknown, assumed in the hundreds. After they resisted Spanish forces, Cortes killed many of them, and branded those he didn't kill.

- **Noche Triste (Sad Night):** After being invited into the king's castle as a guest, Cortes witnessed the king "allegedly" be killed by a rock thrown by an angry citizen. His death, to this day, is debated. Regardless of what really happened, Cortes was convinced the Aztec people would blame him and therefore try to kill him. He was correct. After taking the princess and several nobles as hostages, he and his men escaped from the castle on horseback, lighting the city of Tenochtitlan on fire as they fled. This fire led to an untold number of deaths, possibly in the thousands.

As horrifying as these massacres were, this was only the beginning. *Millions* of people would die over the next 100 years due to famine, disease, and colonial exploitation. It is estimated that, in the 100 years that followed the Spanish arrival, the population in Mesoamerica went from twenty-five million down to under two million.

CHAPTER 30
THEY THOUGHT THEY WERE GODS (EXCEPT THEY DIDN'T)

Let's talk about the silliest colonizer lie ever told: the Aztec thought the Spaniards were gods. Now, this one is so easily disprovable, it's wild to think it got as far as it did. Hernan Cortes kept a journal of everything he did and everything that happened. Others around him did the same, as did the Indigenous people. No one, not the priests or soldiers or Cortes himself made this claim that the Aztec thought he was a god. If no one wrote it down, then why does anyone believe it? Well, in 1552, thirty years *after* the Aztec-Spanish War, a Spanish priest named Francisco López de Gómara was recounting the events of the war. A war he did not witness himself. In fact, he never even set foot in the "New

World." He read through the letters of Cortes and found the following event:

When Cortes landed in what is now Mexico and met the Aztec, they greeted him by "cleansing" him with flowers, perfumes, and more. The priest took this as the natives acknowledging Cortes as a god. The truth is much more embarrassing. Europeans at the time were not known for having the best hygiene, whereas the Aztec bathed daily. When the Aztec met the Spaniards, the Spaniards *stank*. The Aztec "cleansed" them so they didn't smell. That was it.

Did the Aztec sacrifice people? Absolutely. Does this make them savages? No way. But why do we think that? Well, if you wiped out about 90 percent of a population, you want everyone to think you're the good guys. This is the case of the Spaniards; they rewrote history to make themselves not villains, but heroes. They didn't "invade" Mesoamerica, they "freed" it. They didn't burn and kill children, they "ended the tyranny of the Indigenous cannibals." They didn't "destroy gold monuments and melt the gold down for greed," they "brought God to the savages." This is how colonization works. You don't just want everyone to think you're the good guys, you want everyone to think the people you're killing are the bad guys.

CHAPTER 31
MYTHOLOGY THAT CONTRADICTS

Speaking of mythology, there is a lot of contradictory information when it comes to the Aztec. Why? Two reasons. The first is that the Spanish government and the Catholic Church did a hell of a job destroying and rewriting the mythology. Anything that mentioned the following was destroyed: homosexuality, war, sacrifice, gender norms, gambling, religion, gods, etc. Lucky for us, some priests, against the advice of the Church, chose to keep the information, often hiding it away. Other times, the Church just didn't do a good job of removing the information. Whatever the reason, there is a lot of stuff we simply do not know—possibly will never know—because the information was destroyed.

The second reason is on the back of the Aztec. When the Aztec conquered a nation, they didn't demand that the nation stop worshipping their gods. Instead, they said, "Worship your gods and our gods." Once hundreds of nations had been conquered, this meant there were hundreds of variations of the Aztec gods. This is how some characters are sometimes seen as brothers, other times as the same person, other times as completely unrelated. Some characters are husband and wife, other times they are brother and sister, and a few times they are both!

Add to that the fact that a majority of Aztec gods aren't even originals (many were taken from other nations, especially from the Maya). Most gods were repurposed and renamed to fit Aztec mythology. Quetzalcoatl, for instance, is not technically an Aztec god. He is the Feathered Serpent, an ancient being that is found all over Mesoamerica, and the Caribbean, and in nearly every religion.

When you read this book, I promise you that something you read here will be contradicted somewhere else. I have, to the best of my ability, found the stories I feel fit the overall narrative and structure of the Aztec mythology best. This isn't me making things up; this is me painstakingly looking over various sources and deciding which works "best."

CHAPTER 32
LEARNING THE LANGUAGE

The Aztec, or Mexica, spoke the language called Nahuatl. This was the predominant language of the land, the people of the entire land being called the Nahua people. Not to be confused with the Nahual, who were shapeshifters.

X. Hu. Tl. Those letters have been the bane of your existence when trying to say Aztec names, and you will now conquer them! It's actually really easy, once you get the hang of it.

X = Sh, as in "ship."

Xipe = [Ship-eh] This means "to flay" or "peel the skin off."

Hu = W, as in "water."

Huitzil = [Wit-zil] This is a hummingbird.

Tl = T, like the T in "atlas."

Coatl = [Co-ought] This is a snake.

Let's practice some words together!

Atl = [At] This is the word for water.

Xolotl = [Show-low't] This is the word for monster, dog, hairless, deformed, twin.

Axolotl = [Ash-o-low't] This is Atl and Xolotl put together. Axolotl. Water monster.

Xochitl = [Show-cheet] This is the word for flower or beautiful.

Now, let's try to pronounce some bigger names! And just remember, most names of Aztec gods are just two words, side by side. When you see words like Huitzilopochtli, Quetzalcoatl, or Mictecacihuatl, just remember, these are just two words side by side!

Huitzilopochtli = Huitzil + Opochtli

Huitzil = Hummingbird

Opochtli = From the South, or the Left

Huitzilopochtli = The Hummingbird from the South

Quetzalcoatl = Quetzal + Coatl

Chapter 32: Learning the Language

Quetzal = Feather

Coatl = Snake

Quetzalcoatl = Feathered Snake

Mictecacihuatl = Micteca + Cihuatl

Tlaltecuhtli = Tla + Tecuhtli

Tla = Earth/ Stone

Tecuhtli = Lord, or Lord Of

Tlatecuhtli = Stone Lord, or Lord of Earth

The beauty of Aztec gods is that their names often have subtle double meanings.

Huitzilopochtli means the Hummingbird of the South. The Aztec believed that when warriors died, they'd come back to life as hummingbirds. This makes sense, as Huitzilopochtli is the Aztec God of War. But what's with "from the South/ Left?" The South/Left was seen as bad or violent. Think of it like superstition. If you shake hands, you shake with your right hand. Shaking with the left hand is bad luck. The Aztec felt the same. Therefore, he's not just the Hummingbird of the South, he's the Warrior who is violent.

Quetzalcoatl means Feathered Serpent, but both those words have double meanings, and together, they have yet another meaning. Quetzal doesn't just mean "feather," it also means "wise." Which makes sense, Quetzalcoatl is the God of Wisdom. Coatl doesn't just mean "snake," it means eternal. Which, once again, makes sense, as Quetzalcoatl has eternal power. Together, Quetzalcoatl doesn't just mean Feathered Serpent, it means the Wise Eternal or the Eternally Wise. Meaning, not only is he wise, he's infinitely wise.

Tlaltecuhtli isn't just the Lord of Earth, she's the *literal* Earth. What's more, Tlaltecuhtli is one of several examples of Aztec gods who did not follow gender norms.

See, in Aztec society, there are gender-normative titles. Tecuhtli means "Lord," Cihuatl means "Lady." For example, the king and queen of the underworld (Mictlan) are Mictlantecuhtli and Mictecacihuatl. Mictlantecuhtli is the Lord of Mictlan and his wife is Mictecacihuatl, the Lady of the Dead. The non-gender-specific version of Tecuhtli or Cihuatl is Pilli or Teotl. *Pilli* means "prince/princess/ noble." *Teotl* means "god" or "spirit."

Tlatecuhtli does things a little differently, because while Tlaltecuhtli is a woman, she identifies as a man. She is always depicted with breasts and a vagina. She is part of the female-only group known as the Tonantzin. She is, for all intents and purposes, a woman. However, her name has a male title in it: Tecuhtli. This means that she, in some capacity, identifies as a man. Or, at the very least, identifies as gender fluid.

And no, she's not the only one who doesn't follow gender norms. Ometeotl, the creator of the Aztec gods, is both a man and a woman. Ome Teotl means "Two God." They are the duality of the world. Man and woman. Life and Death. Good and evil. Xochipilli, the Flower Prince, is the God of Gay Men. His twin, Xochiquetzal, the Flower Feather, is the Goddess of Lesbians. Tezcatlipoca, the God of Shadows, Magic, Masculinity, etc., has literally hundreds of forms, several of which are women. Tezcatlipoca and Xochiquetzal eventually become husband and wife.

This is all to say, Aztec mythology is different from what you might be used to. Keep an open mind, have fun, and enjoy!

CONCLUSION

What you just read wasn't just a list of gods or some ancient timeline. It was a story that's close to my heart.

Growing up, we hear a lot about other mythologies, but rarely is there a chance to read Aztec mythology in full. Like you, I've always loved Greek, Egyptian, and Norse mythology. I love seeing them in books, in movies, in video games. But as someone who is Latino, that kind of representation was never really there for us.

With this book, my hope is that someone, somewhere, reads it, gets inspired, and expands on the idea. Maybe you'll write your own version! Maybe you'll draw the gods and monsters and make something beautiful and epic! Maybe you'll teach others what you learned, or maybe just carry the stories in your heart. To me, that's the most important thing, because it is how mythology survives. Mythology doesn't survive by staying the same, but by growing with those who carry it.

Stories and characters change and get reinterpreted, or misunderstood, or finally understood for the first time. Mythology, just like history, isn't stagnant. It grows, it changes, and how we view it is always different.

I know it sounds silly to say history changes, because what happened happened and there's no going back. But that's not quite how history works. It's not a singular event, it's a moment with a thousand more moments before and after, all with different points of view. We are always learning more, always finding out more.

To be part of something like that, to me, is a dream come true. To be able to write this story, inspired by the mythology and my own imagination, and present it to you? That's something that'll be a smile on my face for the rest of my life.

Now, to be clear, I'm not the first person to write about Aztec mythology. There are books out there that have done similar things. Not many, but a few. The issue is that, unlike this book, those books were written from one of two angles:

Either the book is a world inspired by Aztec mythology, often very loosely, in which the writer has to do very little research. That way, when something is outright wrong, they can say, "Well, it's my own version." Great for fiction, bad for those trying to learn Aztec mythology.

The other view is often voiced by outsiders or by people trying to make the stories fit into a European or Catholic worldview. These people think sacrificing human beings made the Aztec barbarians, and that opinion carries over into their retelling of it all. I'm not saying sacrifice is or isn't "bad," I'm saying that cultural relativism is important, and I assure you, for all the "awful" stuff the Aztec did, a thousand other nations have done just as bad or worse.

Then there's my book, a painstaking retelling of mythology, kept as close to the truth as possible, while at the same time keeping you, the reader, entertained. Which, if you're reading this, I'm assuming and hoping I achieved.

Still, this book is missing details, and I'm sure if I spent a lifetime researching more, I'd find more to add, but the sad truth is that a lot of the details are gone. Lost to time. Burned during conquest. Forgotten during colonization. Replaced by something easier to control. Yet, despite all that, the stories still exist—and I think that's the most important thing.

These mythologies have survived near-extinction, and it was no easy feat. Still, they live on. They live on in oral tradition, in artwork, in ritual, and in memory. Not just across Mexico, but all over the world. I've talked to people in Japan, Sweden, and Ethiopia who are all fans of Aztec mythology. Which is the point I really want to hammer home: Aztec mythology is not just for Latinos, it's for everyone.

It's with that in mind that we get to this book: my version of Aztec mythology. It's a retelling built from research, intuition, and heart. It is one storyteller's attempt to breathe life back into something that was never supposed to die. I don't claim that this is the only way to tell these stories. But I do believe this version honors the spirit of the original myths, even when the details are incomplete.

In writing this book, I wanted you to feel what it was like to not just read Aztec mythology, but experience it. That's what drew me into writing this book—to not just tell you about mythology, but help you feel for it. I want you to understand that, as with every pantheon, the Aztec gods weren't perfect or untouchable or without fault. In this particular book, we see, even before the first world began, there were mistakes being made. And if gods can make mistakes and be the better for it, so can you. I promise you, when this book series is done, you will be overjoyed and inspired to see how far some of these gods have come.

To me, that's what makes this mythology so powerful. There is, buried somewhere deep within the mythology, a beautiful story waiting to be told.

If you're someone with roots in this culture, I hope this gave you something to hold onto. Something that feels familiar, even if you've never read it before. A piece of yourself you didn't know you were missing.

If you're new to these myths, I hope they opened your eyes. I hope they made you curious. I hope they made you ask questions. Maybe even made you uncomfortable in the best way. That's what good mythology does. It makes you feel something. It stays with you.

While this book is now over, this book series is just beginning. The First Sun hasn't even risen yet and already there's been violence and monsters and war, and I assure you, it's only going to get crazier!

The stories are far from over.
More gods are coming.
Wars will be fought.
Worlds will end.
Have a magical day, everyone!

ABOUT THE AUTHOR

Matthew Torres is a writer, content creator, and storyteller whose work bridges folklore, mythology, and horror with a fresh and fearless voice. Best known as "The Story Time Guy" on TikTok and Instagram, where he has built a loyal audience of nearly half a million followers, he specializes in breathing new life into old legends, especially those too often overlooked.

As a Latino author with deep love and appreciation for Mesoamerican mythology, Torres crafts narratives that reclaim and reimagine ancient stories with authenticity, grit, and heart. His debut book, *Myths, Gods, and Rituals of Aztec Mythology*, offers a sweeping, dramatized retelling of the Aztec mythos for modern audiences.

Beyond books, Torres is actively developing comic books, original films, and story concepts that merge ancient folklore with a modern audience. Whether through myth, monsters, or magical realism, he is committed to telling stories that challenge expectations and give voice to cultural legacies.

He lives in Los Angeles, California, with his wife, Bella; two sons, Peter and Miles; and his two dogs, Gurgi and Padfoot.

Mango Publishing, established in 2014, publishes an eclectic list of books by diverse authors—both new and established voices—on topics ranging from business, personal growth, women's empowerment, LGBTQ studies, health, and spirituality to history, popular culture, time management, decluttering, lifestyle, mental wellness, aging, and sustainable living. We were named 2019 *and* 2020's #1 fastest growing independent publisher by *Publishers Weekly*. Our success is driven by our main goal, which is to publish high-quality books that will entertain readers as well as make a positive difference in their lives.

Our readers are our most important resource; we value your input, suggestions, and ideas. We'd love to hear from you— after all, we are publishing books for you!

Please stay in touch with us and follow us at:

Facebook: Mango Publishing
Twitter: @MangoPublishing
Instagram: @MangoPublishing
LinkedIn: Mango Publishing
Pinterest: Mango Publishing
Newsletter: mangopublishinggroup.com/newsletter

Join us on Mango's journey to reinvent publishing, one book at a time.

www.ingramcontent.com/pod-product-compliance
Lightning Source LLC
Chambersburg PA
CBHW011550070526
44585CB00023B/2528